EXTRAORDI............
NURSES
THROUGHOUT HISTORY

IN HONOUR OF
FLORENCE NIGHTINGALE

By

VARIOUS

"Lo! in that house of misery,
A lady with a lamp I see,
Pass through the glimmering gloom,
And flit from room to room."

LONGFELLOW

CONTENTS

5

CLARA BARTON

SARAH EMMA EDMONDS

LINDA RICHARDS

EDITH CAVELL

VIOLETTA THURSTAN

FOREWORD

From time immemorial women have been content to be as those who serve. *Non ministrari sed ministrare*—not to be ministered unto but to minister—is not alone the motto of those who stand under the Wellesley banner, but of true women everywhere.

For centuries a woman's own home had not only first claim, but full claim, on her fostering care. Her interests and sympathies— her mother love—belonged only to those of her own household. In the days when much of the labor of providing food and clothing was carried on under each roof-tree, her service was necessarily circumscribed by the home walls. Whether she was the lady of a baronial castle, or a hardy peasant who looked upon her work within doors as a rest from her heavier toil in the fields, the mother of the family was not only responsible for the care of her children and the prudent management of her housekeeping, but she had also entire charge of the manufacture of clothing, from the spinning of the flax or wool to the fashioning of the woven cloth into suitable garments.

Changed days have come, however, with changed ways. The development of science and invention, which has led to industrial progress and specialization, has radically changed the woman's world of the home. The industries once carried on there are now more efficiently handled in large factories and packing-houses. The care of the house itself is undertaken by specialists in cleaning and repairing.

Many women, whose energies would have been, under former conditions, inevitably monopolized by home-keeping duties, are to-day giving their strength and special gifts to social service.

They are the true mothers—not only of their own little brood—but of the community and the world.

The service of the true woman is always "womanly." She gives something of the fostering care of the mother, whether it be as nurse, like Clara Barton; as teacher, like Mary Lyon and Alice Freeman Palmer; or as social helper, like Jane Addams. So it is that the service of these "heroines" is that which only women could have given to the world.

Many women who have never held children of their own in their arms have been mothers to many in their work. It was surely the mother heart of Frances E. Willard that made our "maiden crusader" a helper and healer, as well as a standard bearer. It was the mother heart of Alice C. Fletcher, that made that student of the past a champion of the Indians in their present-day problems and a true "campfire interpreter." It was the woman's tenderness that made Mary Slessor, that torch-bearer to Darkest Africa, the "white mother" of all the black people she taught and served.

The Russian peasants have a proverb: "Labor is the house that Love lives in." The women, who, as mothers of their own families, or of other children whose needs cry out for their understanding care, are always homemakers. And the work of each of these—her labor of love—is truly "a house that love lives in."

MARY R. PARKMAN

REPRESENTATIVE WOMEN

THE FREE NURSE

By Ingleby Scott

By the Free Nurse I mean to indicate the Sister of Charity who devotes herself to the sick for their own sake, and from a natural impulse of benevolence, without being bound by any vow or pledge, or having any regard to her own interests in connexion with her office.

There is no dispute about the beauty and excellence of the nursing institutions of the continent, Catholic and Protestant. There can be no doubt that many lives are utilised by them, which would otherwise be frittered away from want of pursuit and guidance. Every town where they live can tell what the blessing is of such a body of qualified nurses, ready to answer any call to the sick-bed. The gratitude of their patients, and the respect of the whole community, testify to their services and merits: and the frequent proposal of some experiment to naturalise such institutions in England, proves that we English are sensible of the beauty of such an organisation of charity. My present purpose, however, is to speak of a more distinctive kind of woman than those who are under vows. However sincere the compassion, however disinterested the devotedness, in an incorporated Sister of Charity, she lies under the disadvantage of her bonds in the first place, and her promised rewards in the other. She may now and then forget her bonds; and there are occasions when they may be a support and relief to her; but they keep her down to the level of an organisation which can never be of a high character while the duty to be performed is regarded as the purchase-money of future benefits to the doer. Those who desire to establish the highest order of nursing had rather see a spontaneous nurse weeping over the body of a suffering child that has gone to its rest than a vowed Sister wiping away the death-damps and closing the eyes, under the promise of a certain amount of remission of sins in consequence. There is abundance of room in society for both vowed and spontaneous nurses, in almost any number; but, their quality as nurses being equal, the strongest interest and affection will always follow the freer, more natural, and more certainly disinterested service. The weaker sort are perhaps wise to put themselves under the orders of authority, which will settle their duty for them: but such cannot be representative women, except by some force of character which in so far raises them above the region of authority. The Representative Women among Nurses are those who have done the duty under some natural incitement, of their own free will, and in their own way.

It will not be supposed, for a moment, that I am speaking slightingly of such organisation as is necessary for the orderly and complete fulfilment of the nursing function. In every hospital where nurses enter freely, and can leave at pleasure, there must be strict rules, settled methods, and a complete organisation of the body of nurses, or all will go into confusion. The authority I refer to as a lower sanction than personal free disposition, is that of religious superiors, who impose the task of nursing as a part of the exercises by which future rewards are to be purchased. There cannot be a more emphatic pleader for hospital and domestic organisation, as a means to the best care of the sick, than Florence Nightingale: and at the same time, all the world knows that she would expect better things from women who become nurses of their own accord, and remain so, through all pains and penalties, when they might give it up at any hour, than from nuns who enter that path of life because it leads (as they believe) straightest to heaven, and do every act at the bidding of a conscience-keeper who holds the ultimate rewards in his hand.

The three women whose honoured names acted singly and spontaneously in devoting themselves to the sick, though their freedom was not of the same character, and their incitements were not alike. Not the less are they all representatives of the growing order of Free Nurses.

On this day two hundred years, Catherine Mompesson was beautiful girl of twenty, near her marriage with a clergyman, who was to introduce her to the life of a minister's wife in a wild place, and among wild people. Their home was the Tillage of Eyam, in Derbyshire, then thickly peopled with miners. In the green dell, and on the breezy hills below and above Eyam, they and their children enjoyed country health and pleasures for a little while. Then the news came of the Great Plague in London; and then of its spreading through the country: but the place was so breezy and so retired, that there might be hope of its being spared the visitation. The winter came, and thanksgivings were fervent for the health the people of Eyam had enjoyed. In the spring, however, when nobody was thinking of dreading the plague, it broke out in the village. Tradition says, it was from some clothes that arrived from a distant place. As soon as it appeared that the mischief was past arresting, the young mother thought first of her children,—or at least, pleaded first for them, in imploring her husband to leave the place with his family. He knew his duty too well. He was firm about remaining; and his desire was that she should carry away her children to a place of safety, than remain there. This she refused with equal firmness: so they sent away the children, and set to work to nurse all Eyam. Out of seventy-six families, two hundred and fifty-nine persons died. The pastor and his wife shut themselves up with the people, allowing nobody to come in or go out, in order to confine the calamity to the village. By his faculty of organisation, all were fed; and by her devotedness, all were nursed, as far as seemed possible, till she sank in the midst of them. Her husband in good time engaged the country people of the surrounding districts to leave food and other supplies at stated places on the hills at fixed hours, when he pledged himself that they should encounter nobody from the village; and these supplies were fetched away at intermediate hours, without any one person ever taking advantage of the opportunity to get away. There could be no stronger evidence of the hold their pastor had on their affections. In a number of the Gentleman's Magazine, published about the close of the last century, there is an engraving of a rock, called "Mompesson's Pulpit." It is a natural arch in the rock, near Eyam, where he stood to read prayers and preach during the plague,—the people being ranged on the open hill-side opposite, and within reach of his voice. This was to avoid the risks of collecting together in the church.

Catherine Mompesson nursed her neighbours from early spring till August, when she died. Amidst the appalling sights and sounds, of which her husband's letters convey a dreadful idea, she sustained herself and him, and all about them. His immediate expectation of following her is shown by his letter of the 1st of September to Sir George Saville, about the choice of his successor and the execution of his will: but he lived till his 70th year—still the good clergyman to his life's end.

It was domestic affection, evidently, which threw Catherine Mompesson into the position of a nurse. At first, she would have left the scene of sickness to preserve husband and children. It was for her husband's sake that she remained—remained to be his helper, at any sacrifice to herself. An incident recorded in one of his letters shows the domestic affections strong in death. She had refused the "cordials" he pressed upon her, saying that she could not swallow them; but, on his suggestion of living for their children, she raised herself in bed, and made the effort. She took the medicines; but she was past saving. Her devotedness as a nurse was not impaired, but sanctified, by the influences under which she undertook the work. So the good Howard thought when he went to Eyam, before his last departure from England, to ascertain what details he could of the pestilence, and of the exemplary nurses of the sick. So think those who even yet visit the churchyard among the hills, and find out her grave, with the intimation at the foot of the suddenness of her call hence. "Cave: nescitis horam."

Mary Pickard's good work was of a similar nature; but even more freely undertaken. She was our contemporary, and has been only a few years dead. She was an American, born, I believe, of English parents; and, at any rate, connected with England by many relationships. In her early womanhood she visited England, previous to her marriage with Dr. Henry Ware, afterwards Divinity Professor in Harvard University. Among other relatives, she chose to visit an aunt who had early married below her station, and settled in the village of Osmotherly, on the borders of Yorkshire and Durham. On reaching the place, she found it ravaged by fever, in the way that one reads of in old books, but never dreams of seeing in the present century.

Mary Pickard could nurse. Through life she was a first-rate nurse, ready to undertake any number of patients, and to suffice to them all—having, in addition to her other nursing powers, a singular gift of serenity and cheerfulness. Full primed with these powers, she dismissed her chaise as soon as she saw how matters stood in the village; and there she remained for weeks and months. She shamed the frightened doctor, and sustained the nervous clergyman, and got up an organisation of the few who were well and strong to clean the streets and houses, and bury the dead quickly, and wash the clothes, and fetch the medicines and food. She herself seemed to the dying quite at leisure to wait upon them: yet the whole management, and no little cooking, and the entire attendance upon a large number of households, all down in the fever, rested upon her. Before she came all who were attacked died: from the day of her arrival some began to mend; but the place was nearly depopulated. She is known there by the name of "the Good Lady;" and most of the villagers never inquired about any other name.

Towards the latter end of the visitation, when she had complained of nothing, and was as cheerful as ever, and unsuspected of any capacity of wearing out, she one day sank down on the floor, and could not get up again. "Never mind!" said she. "It is only want of sleep. Just bring me some blankets, and let me lie here, and I shall do very well." And there she lay— when awake giving directions to others about carrying on her work, but generally asleep, day and night. It was long before she could stand; and when she could she was sent away to recruit. Good nursing and comforts soon restored her; and she went to the village as soon as she was allowed. A joyful cry ran from house to house of those which were still inhabited; and the people crowded round the chaise, throwing in little presents which they had prepared for the chance of the Good Lady returning.

Alone she did it!—the nursing of a fever-stricken population, who were prostrated as by the plague. She did it simply because she was wanted. The people—all entire strangers to her, the aunt and all—were sick and dying; and she could not leave them. It never seemed to herself a remarkable act. The fever scene was remarkable; and of this she spoke with earnestness on occasion: but her own share in it was, in her view, a fine piece of experience; so that, if the fever was to happen, she was glad to have been there. She went back to America, married, and brought up her family of children in the simplest way, being only remarkable for her nursing skill, and the number of sick babies she had tended, and the children who had died in her arms, while she had a houseful of her own to attend to. She died of a lingering and painful disorder, some years after her husband. Her cheerfulness never failed; and in making arrangements for her orphan children, she spoke of her approaching departure just as she would of a voyage to Europe by the next steamer. If ever there was a perfect example of a spontaneous, unprofessional nurse, it was she.

Florence Nightingale, however, will be, through all time to come, the Representative Nurse par excellence! In her case it is a special calling, in virtue of natural capacity, moral and intellectual at once. She did not set out from any chosen starting-point. She did not propose to earn her own salvation by a life of good works. She was not incited by visions of a religious life in a favoured monastic community. She did not aspire to take in hand a department of human misery, in order to extinguish it, and then look about to see what particular misery it should be. She does not appear to have had any plans relating to herself at all. Nor was she overtaken by the plague in a village: nor did she overtake a fever in a village in the course of her travels, like her representative sisters of an earlier time: nor did she do the work of the occasion, and re-enter ordinary life as if nothing had happened. Her case is special and singular in every way.

Her childhood and youth were very much like those of little girls who have wealthy parents, and carefully chosen governesses, and good masters, and much travel—in short, all facilities for intellectual cultivation by study and extended intercourse with society, at home and abroad.

The peculiarity in the case of herself and her nearest relatives seems to be their having been reared in an atmosphere of sincerity and freedom—of reality, in fact,—which is more difficult to obtain than might be thought. There was a certain force and sincerity of character in the elder members on both sides of the house which could not but affect the formation of the children's characters; and in this case there was a governess also whose lofty rectitude and immaculate truthfulness commanded the reverence of all who knew her.

In childhood a domestic incident disclosed to the honest-minded little girl what her liking was, and she followed the lead of her natural taste. She took care of all cuts and bruises, and nursed all illness within her reach; and there is always a good deal of these things within the reach of country gentry who are wealthy and benevolent. For the usual term of young-lady life, Florence Nightingale did as other young ladies. She saw Italy, and looked at its monuments; she once went to Egypt and Greece with the Bracebridges: she visited in society, and went to Court. But her heart was not in the apparent objects of her life—not in travel for amusement, nor in art. In literature, books which disclosed life and its miseries, and character with its sufferings, burnt themselves in upon her mind, and created much of her future effort. She was never resorted to for sentiment. Sentimentalists never had a chance with her. Besides that her character was too strong, and its quality too real for any sympathy with shallowness and egotism, she had two characteristics which might well daunt the sentimentalists—her reserve, and her capacity for ridicule. Ill would they have fared who had come to her for responsive sympathies about sentiment, or even real woes in which no practical help was proposed; and there is perhaps nothing uttered by her, from her evidence before the Sanitary Commission for the Army to her recently published "Notes on Nursing," which does not disclose powers of irony which self-regardant persons may well dread.

Such force and earnestness must find or make a career. She evidently believes, as all persons of genius do, that she found it, while others say she made it. Philosophy will hereafter reconcile the two in her case and many others. As a matter of fact, while other young ladies were busy, and perhaps better employed than usual in enjoying the Great Exhibition, she was in the Kaiserswerth Institution, on the Rhine, going through the training for nursing, and investigating the methods of organisation there and elsewhere.

The strongest sensation she perhaps ever excited among her personal acquaintance was when she undertook to set up the Sanitarium in Harley Street, and left home to superintend the establishment. Her first work there was chiefly financial and the powers of administration she manifested were a complete justification of what she had done in leaving her father's house to become what people called the matron of a charity. At first, common-minded people held up hands and eyes as if she had done something almost scandalous. Between that day and this, they must have discovered that she could exalt any function, and that no function could lower her. She rectified the accounts, paid the debts, and brought all round; and she always had leisure to help and comfort the sick ladies in the house. At one time, I remember, there was not a case in the house which was not hopeless; but there was no sign of dismay in Florence Nightingale. She completed her task, showing unconsciously by it how a woman as well as a man may be born to administration and command.

By a sort of treachery only too common in the visitors of celebrated people, we have all seen the letter of Mr. Sidney Herbert, in 1854, entreating Miss Nightingale to go—accompanied by her friends the Bracebridges, who are familiar with life in the East—to Turkey, to minister among the sick and wounded of our army. How soon she was ready, and how she and her band of nurses went, and were just in time to receive the wounded from Inkermann, no Englishman forgets. No man of any nation concerned will ever forget her subsequent services. She had against her not only a chaos of disorder in which to move, and a hell of misery around her to relieve, but special difficulties in the jealousy of the medical officers, the rawness of the nurses so hastily collected, and the incompatibilities of the volunteer ladies who started on the enterprise with her or after her. On the state of the hospitals it can, I hope, never be necessary to enlarge again. We all know how, under her superintendence, places became clean and airy, and persons cleanly, clothed, fed, and afforded some chance of recovery from maladies or wounds. While history abides, the image of Florence Nightingale, lamp in hand, going through miles of beds, night by night, noting every patient as she went, and ministering wherever most wanted, will always glow in men's hearts; and the sayings of the men about her will be traditions for future generations to enjoy.

She did not, like Mrs. Mompesson, sink down and die in the midst of the scene: nor did she, like Mary Pickard, return into ordinary life for the rest of a long career. She was prostrated by the Crimean fever at Balaklava, and carried up to the hospital on the cliffs till she began to mend, when she was taken to sea. She would not come home, because her work at Scutari was not finished. She remained there till the end of the war, by which time she and her military and medical coadjutors had shown what hospitals may be, and how low the rate of mortality of an army may be reduced, even in time of war.

She has never recovered from that fever; and for some years she has been confined by severe and increasing illness. Not the less has she worked, steadily and most efficiently. She cannot fulfil her aim,—of training nurses in an institution of her own, and thus raising up a body of successors. The grateful people of England supplied the means, without her knowledge or desire,— which was the same thing as imposing a new service upon her. She wished to decline it when she found how little likely her health was to improve. Her letter to the trustees of the fund must be fresh in all memories, and the reply of the trustees, who satisfied her that the money was accumulating, and the plan and the public able and willing to wait. If she could not do this particular work, she has done many others. Her written evidence before the Sanitary Commission for the Army is a great work in itself. So are various reforms urged on the military authorities by her and her coadjutors, and now adopted by the War Office. Reforms in the Indian army are about to follow. The lives thus saved no one will attempt to number; and the amount of misery and vice precluded by her scientific humanity is past all estimate.

Her "Notes on Nursing," prepared and issued in illness and pain, are the crowning evidence of what she is and can do. Hitherto we have, I trust, appreciated and honoured her acts: now we are enabled to perceive and appreciate the quality of her mind. It was as certain before as it can ever be, that she must have acquired no little science, in various departments, to produce the effects she wrought: but we see it all now.

We see also, much more clearly than ever, her moral characteristics. I will not describe them when they can be so much better seen in her "Notes on Nursing." Any one who reads those Notes without being moved in the depths of his heart, will not understand the writer of them by any amount of description: and those who have been so moved, do not need and will not tolerate it. The intense and exquisite humanity to the sick, underlying the glorious common sense about affairs, and the stem insight into the weaknesses and the perversions of the healthy, troubled as they are by the sight of suffering, and sympathising with themselves instead of the patient, lay open a good deal of the secret of this wonderful woman's life and power. We begin to see how a woman, anything but robust at any time, may have been able, as well as willing, to undertake whatever was most repulsive and most agonising in the care of wounded soldiers, and crowds of cholera patients. We see how her minute economy and attention to the smallest details are reconcilable with the magnitude of her administration, and the comprehensiveness of her plans for hospital establishments, and for the reduction of the national rate of mortality. As the lives of the sick hang on small things, she is as earnest about the quality of a cup of arrowroot, and the opening and shutting of doors, as about the institution of a service between the commissariat and the regimental, which shall ensure an army against being starved when within reach of food. In the mind of a true nurse, nothing is too great or too small to be attended to with all diligence: and therefore we have seen Florence Nightingale doing, and insisting upon, the right about shirts and towels, spoon-meats and the boiling of rice; and largely aiding in reducing the mortality of the army from nineteen in the thousand to eight, in time of peace.

It is the best possible rebuke to the egotism, or the sentimentality, which has led several ladies to imagine that they could be nurses, without having tried whether they could bear the discipline. Her pure, undisguised common sense, and her keen perception of all deviations from common sense, may have turned back more or fewer women from the nursing vocation: but this is probably an unmixed good; for those who could be thus turned back were obviously unfit to proceed. She is the representative of those only who are nurses; that is, capable of the hardest and highest duties and sacrifices which women can undertake from love to their race.

In the end she will have won over far more than she can have (most righteously and mercifully) discouraged. Generations of women, for centuries to come, will be the better, the more helpful, and the more devoted for Florence Nightingale having lived; and no small number of each generation will try their strength on that difficult path of beneficence which she has opened, and on which her image will for ever stand to show the way.

INGLEBY SCOTT,
Once A Week, Volume II, 1860

DOROTHEA DIX

1802 — 1887

DOROTHEA L. DIX

By Frances E. Willard and Mary A. Livermore

Philanthropist and army nurse, born in Hampden, Maine, in 1802, and died in Trenton, New Jersey, 7th July, 1887. Her father, a Boston merchant, died in 1821. and Dorothea started a school for girls in that city.

She became interested in the convicts in State prisons, visited them and worked to secure better treatment for them. Her school work and her philanthropic labors broke down her health in 1833, when she was prostrated by haemorrhages from the lungs. Having inherited a small fortune, she went to Europe for her health. The voyage benefited her, and in 1837 she returned to Boston and renewed her labors for the paupers, lunatics and prisoners, in which she was assisted by Rev. Dr. Channing.

The condition of affairs in the East Cambridge almshouse aroused her indignation, and she set about to secure an improvement in the methods of caring for the insane paupers. She visited every State east of the Rocky Mountains, working with the legislatures to provide for the relief of the wretched inmates of the jails, prisons, alms-houses and asylums. In Indiana, Illinois, North Carolina, New York and Pennsylvania she was especially successful in securing legislative action to establish State lunatic asylums.

In January, 1843, she addressed to the Legislature of Massachusetts a memorial in behalf of the "insane persons confined within this Commonwealth, in cages, closets, cellars, stalls, pens; chained, naked. beaten with rods, and lashed into obedience!" The result was a great improvement.

23

In twenty States she visited asylums, pointed out abuses and suggested reforms. She succeeded in founding thirty-two asylums in the United States, in Canada, Nova Scotia, Guernsey and Rome. She secured the changing of the lunacy laws of Scotland. She went to Europe, and there she visited Paris, Florence, Rome, Athens, Constantinople, Vienna, Moscow and St. Petersburg in search of her wards.

Sensitive and refined, she encountered all kinds of men, penetrated into the most loathsome places and faced cruel sights, that she might render effectual service to men and women in whom the loss of reason had not extinguished the human nature, in which her religious soul always saw the work of God.

The years between her return from Europe and the outbreak of the Civil War Miss Dix spent in confirming the strength of the asylums that had sprung from her labors. On 19th April. 1861. she went to do duty as a nurse in the Union army.

During the war she was chief of the woman nurses, and to her is due the soldiers' monument at Fortress Monroe. She established a life-saving station on Sable Island, and after the war, took up again her asylums, seeking their enlargement, improvement and maintenance.

At eighty years of age a retreat was offered her in the Trenton asylum, which she was want to call her "first-born" child. There, after five years of Suffering; she died. Besides being the author of countless memorials to legislatures on the subject of lunatic asylums. Miss Dix wrote and published anonymously "The Garland of Flora" (Boston, 1829), "Conversations About Common Things," "Alice and Ruth," "Evening Hours" and other books for children, "Prisons and Prison Discipline" (Boston, 1845). and a great number of tracts for prisoners.

A Chapter from
A Woman of the Century, 1893

DOROTHEA LYNDE DIX

By Mary Elvira Elliot

Over a grave in Mount Auburn Cemetery, Massachusetts, the American flag always waves. It is kept there by the Army Nurses' Association of Boston and the Grand Army Post, and its presence fittingly commemorates the service which Dorothea Dix rendered her country in the war of the Rebellion.

Miss Dix was born April 4, 1802, during the temporary residence of her parents, Joseph and Mary (Bigelow) Dix, in Hampden, Maine. She died July 17, 1887, at the State Asylum, Trenton, New Jersey, "one of her hospital homes," where she had been tenderly cared for, a loved and revered guest, in her declining years of exhaustion and pain.

It has been remarked that Miss Dix seems to have inherited the strong points of her character not from her parents, but from her paternal grandparents, Dr. Elijah Dix and his wife, Dorothy Lynde. Her father, Joseph Dix, was a visionary man of delicate health, and died early. Her mother, after the birth of her second son, fell into invalidism, leaving to the child Dorothea the care of her two brothers, a trust she faithfully fulfilled.

The grandfather, Dr. Elijah Dix, of whom Miss Dix always cherished pleasant memories, was located many years as a physician at Worcester, where he is remembered to-day as well developed physically and mentally and in advance of his age in village improvement and educational theories. He was characterized for his bravery, honesty, and patriotism. In 1795 he removed to Boston and established a drug store under Faneuil Hall, and founded in South Boston chemical works for the refining of sulphur and the purifying of camphor. He entered largely into the land speculations in the State of Maine, purchased large tracts of forests, out of which he founded the towns of Dixmont and Dixfield. He died in 1809, his widow surviving him twenty-eight years.

At twelve years of age Dorothea, leaving her home in Worcester, went to live with her grandmother, Madam Dix, in Boston. At fourteen she opened a school for little children in Worcester, which she taught in 1816-17. A number of years later she established in the Dix mansion in Boston a boarding and day school, which she continued successfully for five years, but at the cost of her health. In her school-teaching days Miss Dix wrote several books, mostly for children, one of which, "Conversation on Common Things," reached its sixtieth edition. In the spring of 1836 she broke down completely, and was obliged to give up school-keeping. Going to England for change of scene and rest, she returned to Boston in the autumn of 1837 with her health greatly improved, but found it necessary to go South for the following winter. She had received from her grandmother a bequest which, with what she had saved from her earnings as a teacher, gave her a competency, enabling her henceforth to dispose of her time and follow her tastes as she would.

She chose to be a worker in a much neglected field of philanthropy. Visiting in March, 1841, the jail in East Cambridge, "Miss Dix," says her biographer, "was first brought face to face with the condition of things prevailing in the jails and almshouses of Massachusetts, which launched her on her great career."

Note-book in hand, she visited jails and alms-houses throughout the State, accumulating statistics of outrage and misery, and then addressed a memorial to the Legislature (January, 1843), showing the need of reform in the system and appealing for legislative action. She was supported by such men as Dr. Samuel G. Howe, Horace Mann, Charles Sumner, and Dr. Channing. The committee to which the memorial was referred made a report strongly indorsing the truth of

Miss Dix's statements; and engineered by Dr. Howe, chairman of the committee, a "bill for immediate relief was carried by a large majority, and the order passed for providing State accommodations for two hundred additional insane persons."

"Thus was ventured and won Miss Dix's first legislative victory, the precursor of numbers to follow throughout the length and breadth of the United States."

A small asylum in Providence, Rhode Island, receiving from Mr. Cyrus Butler, in answer to a personal appeal from Miss Dix, the sum of fifty thousand dollars, was enlarged and had its name changed to Butler Hospital.

Taking up the cause of the insane in New Jersey, Miss Dix went from county to county, making personal investigations, preparing a memorial to the Legislature, and moving them to appropriate means for building the Trenton Hospital with its lofty walls and extensive grounds. At the same time she was creating the State Lunatic Asylum at Harrisburg, Pennsylvania. Through her efforts the asylum at Utica, New York, was doubled in size, and the asylum for the Insane at Toronto, Canada, tripled. From State to State, from county to county, Miss Dix journeyed, seeking out the suffering in jails, almshouses, and wherever they were to be found, Hospitals sprung up at her touch, until she saw structures of her own creation rise in Illinois, Kentucky, Tennessee, Missouri, Mississippi, Louisiana, Alabama, South Carolina, North Carolina, Maryland, Washington, and Halifax, Nova Scotia.

Far-away Japan owed its first asylum for the insane to Dorothea L. Dix. She so interested Mr. Mori, the first Minister from Japan to the United States, that on his return to his home he was instrumental in building two hospitals.

She was known and loved everywhere. In 1958 and 1959 she visited the hospitals throughout the South that she had been instrumental in founding. She writes in Texas: ' Everybody was kind and obliging. I had a hundred instances that filled my eyes with tears. I was taking dinner at a small public house on a wide, lonely prairie. The master stood with the stage way-bill in his hand, reading and eying me. I thought because I was the only lady passenger; but when I drew out my purse to pay, as usual, his quick expression was: "No, no! by George, I don't take money from you! Why, I never thought I should see you, and now you are in my house. You have done good to everybody for years and years. Make sure, now, there's a welcome for you in every house in Texas! Here, wife, this is Miss Dix. Shake hands and call the children."'

The same kindly spirit was manifested by the press of the South, which spoke of her as ' the chosen daughter of the Republic,' that 'angel of mercy.'

It was during this period of her life that Miss Dix through legislative bodies secured large sums of money for humane purposes, more than was ever before raised by one individual.

At the breaking out of the Civil War, Miss Dix was nearly sixty years of age, but she entered Washington with the first wounded soldiers from Baltimore, and reported at once to Secretary Cameion as a volunteer nurse without pay, and was by him acquitted ' Super- intendent of Women Nurses, to select and assign women nurses to general or inspecting military hospitals.'

"While in personal devotion," writes Mr. Tiffany of Miss Dix (then under the burden of responsibilities too great for any single mind to cope with), "no portion of her career surpassed this, still in wisdom and practical efficiency it was distinctively inferior to her work in her own sphere. Of its consecration of purpose there can be no question." Mr. Tiffany testifies that through the four years of the war "she never took a day's furlough. Untiringly did she remain at her post, organizing bands of nurses, forwarding supplies, inspecting hospitals, and in many a case of neglect and abuse making her name a salutary terror."

Secretary Stanton, having a high sense of the country's indebtedness to Miss Dix for her inestimable services on the battle-field, in camps and hospitals, ordered the presentation to her of a stand of the United States colors. The beautiful flags, received by her in January, 1867, she bequeathed to Harvard College. They now hang in the Memorial Hall, over the main portal.

After the war Miss Dix continued general philanthropic work for many years. Worn out with fatigue, in October, 1881, she went for rest to the Trenton Asylum, which was her home till the end came.

It has been said of Miss Dix that personally she was most attractive. Her voice was of a quality that controlled the rudest and most violent — sweet, lich, low, perfect in enunciation, pervaded in every tone by love and power. Her apparel was quiet, spotlessly neat, and uniquely tasteful — the apparel of a delicate, high-bred Friend. A plain gray dress sufficed for travelling, a black silk one was reserved for social and public occasions. A shawl or velvet mantle without ornament she donned when she went to meet persons of high rank. Her waving brown hair was brought over the temples and carried above the ears, in the fashion of the period. Her soft, brilliant, blue-gray eyes, with pupils so dilating as to make them appear black, the bright glow of her cheeks, the well- set head, and distinction in carriage, all expressed the blending of dignity, force, and tenderness in her character.

A CHAPTER FROM
Representative Women of New England, 1904

MARY SEACOLE

1805 — 1881

A VICTORIAN HEROINE

Excerpts of Chapters from
Adventures of Mrs. Seacole in Many Lands, 1857

By Mary Seacole

I was born in the town of Kingston, in the island of Jamaica, some time in the present century. As a female, and a widow, I may be well excused giving the precise date of this important event. But I do not mind confessing that the century and myself were both young together, and that we have grown side by side into age and consequence. I am a Creole, and have good Scotch blood coursing in my veins. My father was a soldier, of an old Scotch family; and to him I often trace my affection for a camp-life, and my sympathy with what I have heard my friends call "the pomp, pride, and circumstance of glorious war." Many people have also traced to my Scotch blood that energy and activity which are not always found in the Creole race, and which have carried me to so many varied scenes: and perhaps they are right. I have often heard the term "lazy Creole" applied to my country people; but I am sure I do not know what it is to be indolent. All my life long I have followed the impulse which led me to be up and doing; and so far from resting idle anywhere, I have never wanted inclination to rove, nor will powerful enough to find a way to carry out my wishes. That these qualities have led me into many countries, and brought me into some strange and amusing adventures. Some people, indeed, have called me quite a female Ulysses. I believe that they intended it as a compliment; but from my experience of the Greeks, I do not consider it a very flattering one.

It is not my intention to dwell at any length upon the recollections of my childhood. My mother kept a boarding-house in Kingston, and was, like very many of the Creole women, an admirable doctress; in high repute with the officers of both services, and their wives, who were from time to time stationed at Kingston. It was very natural that I should inherit her tastes; and so I had from early youth a yearning for medical knowledge and practice which has never deserted me. When I was a very young child I was taken by an old lady, who brought me up in her household among her own grandchildren, and who could scarcely have shown me more kindness had I been one of them; indeed, I was so spoiled by my kind patroness that, but for being frequently with my mother, I might very likely have grown up idle and useless. But I saw so much of her, and of her patients, that the ambition to become a doctress early took firm root in my mind; and I was very young when I began to make use of the little knowledge I had acquired from watching my mother, upon a great sufferer—my doll. I have noticed always what actors children are. If you leave one alone in a room, how soon it clears a little stage; and, making an audience out of a few chairs and stools, proceeds to act its childish griefs and blandishments upon its doll. So I also made good use of my dumb companion and confidante; and whatever disease was most prevalent in Kingston, be sure my poor doll soon contracted it. I have had many medical triumphs in later days, and saved some valuable lives; but I really think that few have given me more real gratification than the rewarding glow of health which my fancy used to picture stealing over my patient's waxen face after long and precarious illness.

Before long it was very natural that I should seek to extend my practice; and so I found other patients in the dogs and cats around me. Many luckless brutes were made to simulate diseases which were raging among their owners, and had forced down their reluctant throats the remedies which I deemed most likely to suit their supposed complaints. And after a time I rose still higher in my ambition; and despairing of finding another human patient, I proceeded to try my simples and essences upon—myself.

When I was about twelve years old I was more frequently at my mother's house, and used to assist her in her duties; very often sharing with her the task of attending upon invalid officers or their wives, who came to her house from the adjacent camp at Up-Park, or the military station at Newcastle.

As I grew into womanhood, I began to indulge that longing to travel which will never leave me while I have health and vigour. I was never weary of tracing upon an old map the route to England; and never followed with my gaze the stately ships homeward bound without longing to be in them, and see the blue hills of Jamaica fade into the distance. At that time it seemed most improbable that these girlish wishes should be gratified; but circumstances, which I need not explain, enabled me to accompany some relatives to England while I was yet a very young woman.

I shall never forget my first impressions of London. Of course, I am not going to bore the reader with them; but they are as vivid now as though the year 18— (I had very nearly let my age slip then) had not been long ago numbered with the past. Strangely enough, some of the most vivid of my recollections are the efforts of the London street-boys to poke fun at my and my companion's complexion. I am only a little brown—a few shades duskier than the brunettes whom you all admire so much; but my companion was very dark, and a fair (if I can apply the term to her) subject for their rude wit. She was hot-tempered, poor thing! and as there were no policemen to awe the boys and turn our servants' heads in those days, our progress through the London streets was sometimes a rather chequered one.

I remained in England, upon the occasion of my first visit, about a year; and then returned to Kingston. Before long I again started for London, bringing with me this time a large stock of

West Indian preserves and pickles for sale. After remaining two years here, I again started home; and on the way my life and adventures were very nearly brought to a premature conclusion. Christmas-day had been kept very merrily on board our ship the "Velusia;" and on the following day a fire broke out in the hold. I dare say it would have resisted all the crew's efforts to put it out, had not another ship appeared in sight; upon which the fire quietly allowed itself to be extinguished. Although considerably alarmed, I did not lose my senses; but during the time when the contest between fire and water was doubtful, I entered into an amicable arrangement with the ship's cook, whereby, in consideration of two pounds—which I was not, however, to pay until the crisis arrived—he agreed to lash me on to a large hen-coop.

Before I had been long in Jamaica I started upon other trips, many of them undertaken with a view to gain. Thus I spent some time in New Providence, bringing home with me a large collection of handsome shells and rare shell-work, which created quite a sensation in Kingston, and had a rapid sale; I visited also Hayti and Cuba. But I hasten onward in my narrative.

Returned to Kingston, I nursed my old indulgent patroness in her last long illness. After she died, in my arms, I went to my mother's house, where I stayed, making myself useful in a variety of ways, and learning a great deal of Creole medicinal art, until I couldn't find courage to say "no" to a certain arrangement timidly proposed by Mr. Seacole, but married him, and took him down to Black River, where we established a store. Poor man! he was very delicate; and before I undertook the charge of him, several doctors had expressed most unfavourable opinions of his health. I kept him alive by kind nursing and attention as long as I could; but at last he grew so ill that we left Black River, and returned to my mother's house at Kingston. Within a month of our arrival there he died. This was my first great trouble, and I felt it bitterly. For days I never stirred—lost to all that passed around me in a dull stupor of despair. If you had told me that the time would soon come when I should remember this sorrow calmly, I should not have believed it possible: and yet it was so. I do not think that we hot-blooded Creoles sorrow less for showing it so impetuously; but I do think that the sharp edge of our grief wears down sooner than theirs who preserve an outward demeanour of calmness, and nurse their woe secretly in their hearts.

* * * * *

I have attempted, without any consideration of dates, to give my readers some idea of my life in the Crimea. I am fully aware that I have jumbled up events strangely, talking in the same page, and even sentence, of events which occurred at different times; but I have three excuses to offer for my unhistorical inexactness. In the first place, my memory is far from trustworthy, and I kept no written diary; in the second place, the reader must have had more than enough of journals and chronicles of Crimean life, and I am only the historian of Spring Hill; and in the third place, unless I am allowed to tell the story of my life in my own way, I cannot tell it at all.

I shall now endeavour to describe my out-of-door life as much as possible, and write of those great events in the field of which I was a humble witness. But I shall continue to speak from my own experience simply; and if the reader should be surprised at my leaving any memorable action of the army unnoticed, he may be sure that it is because I was mixing medicines or making good things in the kitchen of the British Hotel, and first heard the particulars of it, perhaps, from the newspapers which came from home. My readers must know, too, that they were much more familiar with the history of the camp at their own firesides, than we who lived in it. Just as a spectator seeing one of the battles from a hill, as I did the Tchernaya, knows more about it than the combatant in the valley below, who only thinks of the enemy whom it is his immediate duty to repel; so you, through the valuable aid of the cleverest man in the whole camp, read in the *Times'* columns the details of that great campaign, while we, the actors in it, had enough to do to discharge our own duties well, and rarely concerned ourselves in what seemed of such importance to you. And so very often a desperate skirmish or hard-fought action, the news of which created so much sensation in England, was but little regarded at Spring Hill.

My first experience of battle was pleasant enough. Before we had been long at Spring Hill, Omar Pasha got something for his Turks to do, and one fine morning they were marched away towards the Russian outposts on the road to Baidar. I accompanied them on horseback, and enjoyed the sight amazingly. English and French cavalry preceded the Turkish infantry over the plain yet full of memorials of the terrible Light Cavalry charge a few months before; and while one detachment of the Turks made a reconnaissance to the right of the Tchernaya, another pushed their way up the hill, towards Kamara, driving in the Russian outposts, after what seemed but a slight resistance. It was very pretty to see them advance, and to watch how every now and then little clouds of white smoke puffed up from behind bushes and the crests of hills, and were answered by similar puffs from the long line of busy skirmishers that preceded the main body. This was my first experience of actual battle, and I felt that strange excitement which I do not remember on future occasions, coupled with an earnest longing to see more of warfare, and to share in its hazards. It was not long before my wish was gratified.

I do not know much of the second bombardment of Sebastopol in the month of April, although I was as assiduous as I could be in my attendance at Cathcart's Hill. I could judge of its severity by the long trains of wounded which passed the British Hotel. I had a stretcher laid near the door, and very often a poor fellow was laid upon it, outwearied by the terrible conveyance from the front.

After this unsuccessful bombardment, it seemed to us that there was a sudden lull in the progress of the siege; and other things began to interest us. There were several arrivals to talk over. Miss Nightingale came to supervise the Balaclava hospitals, and, before long, she had practical experience of Crimean fever. After her, came the Duke of Newcastle, and the great high priest of the mysteries of cookery, Mons. Alexis Soyer. He was often at Spring Hill, with the most smiling of faces and in the most gorgeous of irregular uniforms, and never failed to praise my soups and dainties. I always flattered myself that I was his match, and with our West Indian dishes could of course beat him hollow, and more than once I challenged him to a trial of skill; but the gallant Frenchman only shrugged his shoulders, and disclaimed my challenge with many flourishes of his jewelled hands, declaring that Madame proposed a contest where victory would cost him his reputation for gallantry, and be more disastrous than defeat. And all because I was a woman, forsooth. What nonsense to talk like that, when I was doing the work of half a dozen men. Then he would laugh and declare that, when our campaigns were over, we would render rivalry impossible, by combining to open the first restaurant in Europe. There was always fun in the store when the good-natured Frenchman was there.

One dark, tempestuous night, I was knocked up by the arrival of other visitors. These were the first regiment of Sardinian Grenadiers, who, benighted on their way to the position assigned them, remained at Spring Hill until the morning. We soon turned out our staff, and lighted up the store, and entertained the officers as well as we could inside, while the soldiers bivouacked in the yards around. Not a single thing was stolen or disturbed that night, although they had many opportunities. We all admired and liked the Sardinians; they were honest, well-disciplined fellows, and I wish there had been no worse men or soldiers in the Crimea.

As the season advanced many visitors came to the Crimea from all parts of the world, and many of them were glad to make Spring Hill their head-quarters. We should have been better off if some of them had spared us this compliment. A Captain St. Clair, for instance—who could doubt any one with such a name?—stayed some time with us, had the best of everything, and paid us most honourably with one bill upon his agents, while we cashed another to provide him with money for his homeward route. He was an accomplished fellow, and I really liked him; but, unfortunately for us, he was a swindler.

I saw much of another visitor to the camp in the Crimea—an old acquaintance of mine with whom I had had many a hard bout in past times—the cholera. There were many cases in the hospital of the Land Transport Corps opposite, and I prescribed for many others personally. The raki sold in too many of the stores in Balaclava and Kadikoi was most pernicious; and although the authorities forbade the sutlers to sell it, under heavy penalties, it found its way into the camp in large quantities.

During May, and while preparations were being made for the third great bombardment of the ill-fated city, summer broke beautifully, and the weather, chequered occasionally by fitful intervals of cold and rain, made us all cheerful. You would scarcely have believed that the happy, good-humoured, and jocular visitors to the British Hotel were the same men who had a few weeks before ridden gloomily through the muddy road to its door. It was a period of relaxation, and they all enjoyed it. Amusement was the order of the day. Races, dog-hunts, cricket-matches, and dinner-parties were eagerly indulged in, and in all I could be of use to provide the good cheer which was so essential a part of these entertainments; and when the warm weather came in all its intensity, and I took to manufacturing cooling beverages for my friends and customers, my store was always full. To please all was somewhat difficult, and occasionally some of them were scarcely so polite as they should have been to a perplexed hostess, who could scarcely be expected to remember that Lieutenant A. had bespoken his sangaree an instant before Captain B. and his friends had ordered their claret cup.

In anticipation of the hot weather, I had laid in a large stock of raspberry vinegar, which, properly managed, helps to make a pleasant drink; and there was a great demand for sangaree, claret, and cider cups, the cups being battered pewter pots. Would you like, reader, to know my recipe for the favourite claret cup? It is simple enough. Claret, water, lemon-peel, sugar, nutmeg, and—ice—yes, ice, but not often and not for long, for the eager officers soon made an end of it. Sometimes there were dinner-parties at Spring Hill, but of these more hereafter. At one of the earliest, when the *Times* correspondent was to be present, I rode down to Kadikoi, bought some calico and cut it up into table napkins. They all laughed very heartily, and thought perhaps of a few weeks previously, when every available piece of linen in the camp would have been snapped up for pocket-handkerchiefs.

But the reader must not forget that all this time, although there might be only a few short and sullen roars of the great guns by day, few nights passed without some fighting in the trenches; and very often the news of the morning would be that one or other of those I knew had fallen. These tidings often saddened me, and when I awoke in the night and heard the thunder of the guns fiercer than usual, I have quite dreaded the dawn which might usher in bad news.

The deaths in the trenches touched me deeply, perhaps for this reason. It was very usual, when a young officer was ordered into the trenches, for him to ride down to Spring Hill to dine, or obtain something more than his ordinary fare to brighten his weary hours in those fearful ditches. They seldom failed on these occasions to shake me by the hand at parting, and sometimes would say, "You see, Mrs. Seacole, I can't say good-bye to the dear ones at home, so I'll bid you good-bye for them. Perhaps you'll see them some day, and if the Russians should knock me over, mother, just tell them I thought of them all— will you?" And although all this might be said in a light-hearted manner, it was rather solemn. I felt it to be so, for I never failed (although who was I, that I should preach?) to say something about God's providence and relying upon it; and they were very good. No army of parsons could be much better than my sons. They would listen very gravely, and shake me by the hand again, while I felt that there was nothing in the world I would not do for them. Then very often the men would say, "I'm going in with my master to-night, Mrs. Seacole; come and look after him, if he's hit;" and so often as this happened I would pass the night restlessly, awaiting with anxiety the morning, and yet dreading to hear the news it held in store for me. I used to think it was like having a large family of children ill with fever, and dreading to hear which one had passed away in the night.

And as often as the bad news came, I thought it my duty to ride up to the hut of the sufferer and do my woman's work. But I felt it deeply. How could it be otherwise? There was one poor boy in the Artillery, with blue eyes and light golden hair, whom I nursed through a long and weary sickness, borne with all a man's spirit, and whom I grew to love like a fond old-fashioned mother. I thought if ever angels watched over any life, they would shelter his; but one day, but a short time after he had left his sick-bed, he was struck down on his battery, working like a young hero. It was a long time before I could banish from my mind the thought of him as I saw him last, the yellow hair, stiff and stained with his life-blood, and the blue eyes closed in the sleep of death. Of course, I saw him buried, as I did poor H—— V——, my old Jamaica friend, whose kind face was so familiar to me of old. Another good friend I mourned bitterly—Captain B——, of the Coldstreams—a great cricketer. He had been with me on the previous evening, had seemed dull, but had supped at my store, and on the following morning a brother officer told me he was shot dead while setting his pickets, which made me ill and unfit for work for the whole day. Mind you, a day was a long time to give to sorrow in the Crimea.

I could give many other similar instances, but why should I sadden myself or my readers? Others have described the horrors of those fatal trenches; but their real history has never been written, and perhaps it is as well that so harrowing a tale should be left in oblivion. Such anecdotes as the following were very current in the Camp, but I have no means of answering for its truth. Two sergeants met in the trenches, who had been schoolmates in their youth; years had passed since they set out for the battle of life by different roads, and now they met again under the fire of a common enemy. With one impulse they started forward to exchange the hearty hand-shake and the mutual greetings, and while their hands were still clasped, a chance shot killed both.

EXCERPTS OF CHAPTERS FROM
Adventures of Mrs. Seacole in Many Lands, 1857

FLORENCE NIGHTINGALE

1820 — 1910

"THE LADY WITH THE LAMP"

THE STORY OF
FLORENCE NIGHTINGALE

By F. J. Cross

"She would speak to one and another, and nod and smile to many more, but she could not do it to all, you know, for we lay there by hundreds; but we could kiss her shadow as it fell, and lay our heads on our pillows again, content."

So wrote one of the soldiers from the hospital at Scutari of Florence Nightingale, the soldier's nurse, and the soldier's friend.

Let us see how it happened that Florence Nightingale was able to do so much for the British soldiers who fought in the Crimea, and why she has left her mark on the history of our times.

Miss Nightingale was born in the city of Florence in the year 1820, and it is from that beautiful Italian town that she derives her Christian name.

Her father was a good and wealthy man, who took great interest in the poor; and her mother was ever seeking to do them some kindness.

Thus Florence saw no little of cottage folk. She took them dainties when they were ailing, and delighted to nurse them when ill.

She loved all dumb animals, and they seemed to know by instinct that she was their friend. One day she came across her father's old shepherd, looking as miserable as could be; and, on inquiring the cause, found that a mischievous boy had thrown a stone at his favourite dog, which had broken its leg, and he was afraid it would have to be killed.

Going together to the shepherd's home they found the dog very excited and angry; but, on Florence speaking to it in her gentle voice, it came and lay down at her feet, and allowed her to examine the damaged limb.

Happily, she discovered it was only bruised; and she attended to it so skilfully that the dog was soon running about in the field again. A few days later she met the shepherd,—he was simply beaming, for the dog had recovered and was with him.

When Florence spoke to the man the dog wagged its tail as much as to say, "I'm mighty glad to see *you* again"; whereupon the shepherd remarked: "Do look at the dog, miss, he be so pleased to hear your voice".

The fact that even her dolls were properly bandaged when their limbs became broken, or the sawdust began to run out of their bodies, will show that even then she was a thoughtful, kindly little person.

When she grew up she wished very much to learn how to nurse the sick.

But in those days it was not considered at all a ladylike thing to do; and, after trying one or two nursing institutions at home, she went to Germany, and afterwards to Paris, in order to make a study of the subject, and to get practical experience in cities abroad.

Miss Nightingale thus learnt nursing very thoroughly, and when she came back to England turned her knowledge to account by taking charge of an institution in London. By good management, tact and skill, the institution became a great success; but she was too forgetful of self, and after a time the hard work told upon her health, and she was obliged to take a rest from her labours.

The time came when the Russian war broke out and Great Britain and France sent their armies into the Crimea. Our men fought like heroes. But it was found out ere many months had passed that those brave fellows, who were laying down their lives for the sake of their country, were being so badly nursed when they were sick and wounded that more were being slain by neglect than by the guns of the enemy.

Then there arose a great cry in Britain; and every one demanded that something should be done to remedy this state of things. But nobody knew quite what to do or how to do it, except one woman,—and that woman was Florence Nightingale.

Mr. Sidney Herbert, the War Minister, was one of the very few people who knew anything about her great powers of organisation; and happily he did know how thoroughly fit she was for the task of properly directing the nursing of the sick soldiers.

So, on the 15th October, 1854, he asked her to go to the Crimea to take entire charge of the nursing arrangements; and in less than a week she started with about forty nurses for Scutari, the town where the great hospital was situated.

All Britain was stirred with admiration at her heroism; for it was well known how difficult was the task she was undertaking. But the quiet gentle woman herself feared neither death, disease nor hard work; the only thing she did not like was the fuss the people made about her.

Scutari, whither she went, is situated on the eastern side of the Bosphorus, opposite Constantinople. Thither the sick and wounded soldiers were being brought by hundreds. It took four or five days to get them from the field of battle to the hospital, their wounds during that tame being generally unattended to. When they arrived at Scutari, it was difficult to land them; after that there was a steep hill up which they had to be carried to the hospital, so that by the time they arrived they were generally in a sad condition. But their trials were not over then. The hospital was dirty and dismal. There was no proper provision for the supply of suitable food, everything was in dire disorder, and the poor fellows died of fever in enormous numbers.

But "the lady with the lamp" soon brought about a revolution;

and the soldiers knew to their joy what it was to have proper nursing. No wonder the men kissed her shadow! Wherever the worst cases were to be found there was Florence Nightingale. Day and night she watched and waited, worked and prayed. Her very presence was medicine and food and light to the soldiers.

Gradually disorder disappeared, and deaths became fewer day by day. Good nursing; care and cleanliness; nourishing food, and—perhaps beyond and above all—love and tenderness, wrought wonders. The oath in the soldier's mouth turned to a prayer at her appearance.

Though the beds extended over a space equal to four miles, yet each man knew that all that human strength could do to forward his recovery was being done.

Before her task was finished Miss Nightingale had taken the fever herself, but her life was mercifully spared.

Since those days, Florence Nightingale has done many kindly and noble deeds. She has always lived as much out of the public sight as possible, though her work has rendered her dear to all hearts.

Though she has had much ill health herself, she has been able to accomplish a splendid life's work, and to advance the study of nursing in all parts of the globe.

A Chapter from
Beneath the Banner – Being Narratives
of Noble Lives and Brave Deeds, 1894

FLORENCE NIGHTINGALE

By Lytton Strachey

EVERY one knows the popular conception of Florence Nightingale. The saintly, self-sacrificing woman, the delicate maiden of high degree who threw aside the pleasures of a life of ease to succour the afflicted; the Lady with the Lamp, gliding through the horrors of the hospital at Scutari, and consecrating with the radiance of her goodness the dying soldier's couch. The vision is familiar to all—but the truth was different. The Miss Nightingale of fact was not as facile as fancy painted her. She worked in another fashion and towards another end; she moved under the stress of an impetus which finds no place in the popular imagination. A Demon possessed her. Now demons, whatever else they may be, are full of interest. And so it happens that in the real Miss Nightingale there was more that was interesting than in the legendary one; there was also less that was agreeable.

Her family was extremely well-to-do, and connected by marriage with a spreading circle of other well-to-do families. There was a large country house in Derbyshire; there was another in the New Forest; there were Mayfair rooms for the London season and all its finest parties; there were tours on the Continent with even more than the usual number of Italian operas and of glimpses at the celebrities of Paris. Brought up among such advantages, it was only natural to suppose that Florence would show a proper appreciation of them by doing her duty in that state of life unto which it had pleased God to call her—in other words, by marrying, after a fitting number of dances and dinner-parties, an eligible gentleman, and living happily ever afterwards.

Her sister, her cousins, all the young ladies of her acquaintance, were either getting ready to do this or had already done it.

It was inconceivable that Florence should dream of anything else; yet dream she did. Ah! To do her duty in that state of life unto which it had pleased God to call her! Assuredly, she would not be behindhand in doing her duty; but unto what state of life HAD it pleased God to call her? That was the question. God's calls are many, and they are strange. Unto what state of life had it pleased Him to call Charlotte Corday, or Elizabeth of Hungary? What was that secret voice in her ear, if it was not a call? Why had she felt, from her earliest years, those mysterious promptings towards ... she hardly knew what, but certainly towards something very different from anything around her? Why, as a child in the nursery, when her sister had shown a healthy pleasure in tearing her dolls to pieces, had SHE shown an almost morbid one in sewing them up again? Why was she driven now to minister to the poor in their cottages, to watch by sick-beds, to put her dog's wounded paw into elaborate splints as if it was a human being? Why was her head filled with queer imaginations of the country house at Embley turned, by some enchantment, into a hospital, with herself as matron moving about among the beds? Why was even her vision of heaven itself filled with suffering patients to whom she was being useful? So she dreamed and wondered, and, taking out her diary, she poured into it the agitations of her soul. And then the bell rang, and it was time to go and dress for dinner.

As the years passed, a restlessness began to grow upon her. She was unhappy, and at last she knew it. Mrs. Nightingale, too, began to notice that there was something wrong. It was very odd—what could be the matter with dear Flo? Mr. Nightingale suggested that a husband might be advisable; but the curious thing was that she seemed to take no interest in husbands. And with her attractions, and her accomplishments, too! There was nothing in the world to prevent her making a really brilliant match. But no! She would think of nothing but how to satisfy that singular craving of hers to be DOING something. As if there was not plenty to do in any case, in the ordinary way, at home. There was the china to look after, and there was her father to be read to after dinner. Mrs. Nightingale could not understand it; and then one day her perplexity was changed to consternation and alarm. Florence announced an extreme desire to go to Salisbury Hospital for several months as a nurse; and she confessed to some visionary plan of eventually setting up in a house of her own in a neighbouring village, and there founding 'something like a Protestant Sisterhood, without vows, for women of educated feelings'. The whole scheme was summarily brushed aside as preposterous; and Mrs. Nightingale, after the first shock of terror, was able to settle down again more or less comfortably to her embroidery. But Florence, who was now twenty-five and felt that the dream of her life had been shattered, came near to desperation.

And, indeed, the difficulties in her path were great. For not only was it an almost unimaginable thing in those days for a woman of means to make her own way in the world and to live in independence, but the particular profession for which Florence was clearly marked out both by her instincts and her capacities was at that time a peculiarly disreputable one. A 'nurse' meant then a coarse old woman, always ignorant, usually dirty, often brutal, a Mrs. Gamp, in bunched-up sordid garments, tippling at the brandy bottle or indulging in worse irregularities. The nurses in the hospitals were especially notorious for immoral conduct; sobriety was almost unknown among them; and they could hardly be trusted to carry out the simplest medical duties.

Certainly, things HAVE changed since those days; and that they have changed is due, far more than to any other human being, to Miss Nightingale herself. It is not to be wondered at that her parents should have shuddered at the notion of their daughter devoting her life to such an occupation. 'It was as if,' she herself said afterwards, 'I had wanted to be a kitchen-maid.' Yet the want, absurd and impracticable as it was, not only remained fixed immovably in her heart, but grew in intensity day by day. Her wretchedness deepened into a morbid melancholy. Everything about her was vile, and she herself, it was clear, to have deserved such misery, was even viler than her surroundings. Yes, she had sinned—'standing before God's judgment seat'. 'No one,' she declared, 'has so grieved the Holy Spirit'; of that she was quite certain. It was in vain that she prayed to be delivered from vanity and hypocrisy, and she could not bear to smile or to be gay, 'because she hated God to hear her laugh, as if she had not repented of her sin'.

A weaker spirit would have been overwhelmed by the load of such distresses—would have yielded or snapped. But this extraordinary young woman held firm, and fought her way to victory. With an amazing persistency, during the eight years that followed her rebuff over Salisbury Hospital, she struggled and worked and planned. While superficially she was carrying on the life of a brilliant girl in high society, while internally she was a prey to the tortures of regret and of remorse, she yet possessed the energy to collect the knowledge and to undergo the experience which alone could enable her to do what she had determined she would do in the end. In secret she devoured the reports of medical commissions, the pamphlets of sanitary authorities, the histories of hospitals and homes. She spent the intervals of the London season in ragged schools and workhouses. When she went abroad with her family, she used her spare time so well that there was hardly a great hospital in Europe with which she was not acquainted; hardly a great city whose slums she had not passed through.

She managed to spend some days in a convent school in Rome, and some weeks as a 'Soeur de Charite' in Paris. Then, while her mother and sister were taking the waters at Carlsbad, she succeeded in slipping off to a nursing institution at Kaiserswerth, where she remained for more than three months. This was the critical event of her life. The experience which she gained as a nurse at Kaiserswerth formed the foundation of all her future action and finally fixed her in her career.

But one other trial awaited her. The allurements of the world she had brushed aside with disdain and loathing; she had resisted the subtler temptation which, in her weariness, had sometimes come upon her, of devoting her baffled energies to art or literature; the last ordeal appeared in the shape of a desirable young man. Hitherto, her lovers had been nothing to her but an added burden and a mockery; but now—for a moment—she wavered. A new feeling swept over her—a feeling which she had never known before—which she was never to know again. The most powerful and the profoundest of all the instincts of humanity laid claim upon her. But it rose before her, that instinct, arrayed—how could it be otherwise?—in the inevitable habiliments of a Victorian marriage; and she had the strength to stamp it underfoot.

'I have an intellectual nature which requires satisfaction,' she noted, 'and that would find it in him. I have a passionate nature which requires satisfaction, and that would find it in him. I have a moral, an active nature which requires satisfaction, and that would not find it in his life. Sometimes I think that I will satisfy my passionate nature at all events....'

But no, she knew in her heart that it could not be. 'To be nailed to a continuation and exaggeration of my present life ... to put it out of my power ever to be able to seize the chance of forming for myself a true and rich life'—that would be a suicide. She made her choice, and refused what was at least a certain happiness for a visionary good which might never come to her at all. And so she returned to her old life of waiting and bitterness.

'The thoughts and feelings that I have now,' she wrote, 'I can remember since I was six years old. A profession, a trade, a necessary occupation, something to fill and employ all my faculties, I have always felt essential to me, I have always longed for. The first thought I can remember, and the last, was nursing work; and in the absence of this, education work, but more the education of the bad than of the young ... Everything has been tried—foreign travel, kind friends, everything. My God! What is to become of me?'

A desirable young man? Dust and ashes! What was there desirable in such a thing as that? 'In my thirty-first year,' she noted in her diary, 'I see nothing desirable but death.'

Three more years passed, and then at last the pressure of time told; her family seemed to realise that she was old enough and strong enough to have her way; and she became the superintendent of a charitable nursing home in Harley Street. She had gained her independence, though it was in a meagre sphere enough; and her mother was still not quite resigned: surely Florence might at least spend the summer in the country. At times, indeed, among her intimates, Mrs. Nightingale almost wept. 'We are ducks,' she said with tears in her eyes, 'who have hatched a wild swan.' But the poor lady was wrong; it was not a swan that they had hatched, it was an eagle.

A Chapter From
Eminent Victorians, 1918

FLORENCE NIGHTINGALE

By Millicent Fawcett

Among the personal influences that have altered the everyday life of the present century, the future historian will probably allot a prominent place to that of Florence Nightingale. Before she took up the work of her life, the art of sick nursing in England can hardly have been said to exist. Almost every one had a well-founded horror of the hired nurse; she was often ignorant, cruel, rapacious, and drunken; and when she was not quite as bad as that, she was prejudiced, superstitious, and impervious to new ideas or knowledge. The worst type of the nurse of the pre-Nightingale era has been portrayed by Dickens in his "Sairey Gamp" with her bottle of gin or rum upon the "chimbley piece," handy for her to put it to her lips when she was "so dispoged." "Sairey Gamp" is one of the blessings of the good old days which have now vanished for ever; with her disappearance has also gradually disappeared the repugnance with which the professional nurse was at one time almost universally regarded; and there is now hardly any one who has not had cause to be thankful for the quick, gentle, and skilful assistance of the trained nurse whose existence we owe to the example and precepts of Florence Nightingale.

Miss Nightingale has never favoured the curiosity of those who would wish to pry into the details of her private history. She has indeed been so retiring that there is some difficulty in getting accurate information about anything concerning her, with the exception of her public work. In a letter she has allowed to be published, she says, "Being naturally a very shy person, most of my life has been distasteful to me." It would be very ungrateful and unbecoming in those who have benefited by her self-forgetful labours to attempt in any way to thwart her desire for privacy as to her personal affairs. The attention of the readers of this sketch will therefore be directed to Miss Nightingale's public work, and what the world, and women in particular, have gained by the noble example she has set of how women's work should be done.

From time immemorial it has been universally recognised that the care of the sick is women's work; but somehow, partly from the low standard of women's education, partly from the false notion that all paid work was in a way degrading to a woman's gentility, it seemed to be imagined that women could do this work of caring for the sick without any special teaching or preparation for it; and as all paid work was supposed to be unladylike, no woman undertook it unless she was driven to it by the dire stress of poverty, and had therefore neither the time nor means to acquire the training necessary to do it well. The lesson of Florence Nightingale's life is that painstaking study and preparation are just as necessary for women's work as they are for men's work. No young man attempts responsible work as a doctor, a lawyer, an engineer, or even a gardener or mechanic, without spending long years in fitting himself for his work; but in old times women seemed to think they could do all their work, in governessing, nursing, or what not, by the light of nature, and without any special teaching and preparation whatever. There is still some temptation on the part of women to fall into this fatal error. A young woman, not long ago, who had studied medicine in India only two years, was placed at the head of a dispensary and hospital for native women. Who would have dreamt of taking a boy, after only two years' study, for a post of similar responsibility and difficulty? Of course failure and disappointment resulted, and it will probably be a long time before the native community in that part of India recover their confidence in lady doctors.

Miss Nightingale spent nearly ten years in studying nursing before she considered herself qualified to undertake the sanitary direction of even a small hospital. She went from place to place, not confining her studies to her own country. She spent about a year at the hospital and nursing institution at Kaiserswerth on the Rhine in 1849. This had been founded by Pastor Fliedner, and was under the care of a Protestant Sisterhood who had perfected the art of sick nursing to a degree unknown at that time in any other part of Europe. From Kaiserswerth she visited institutions for similar purposes, in other parts of Germany, and in France and Italy. It is obvious she could not have devoted the time and money which all this preparation must have cost if she had not been a member of a wealthy family. The fact that she was so makes her example all the more valuable. She was the daughter and co-heiress of a wealthy country gentleman of Lea Hurst in Derbyshire, and Embly Park in Hampshire. As a young girl she had the choice of all that wealth, luxury, and fashion could offer in the way of self-indulgence and ease, and she set them all on one side for the sake of learning how to benefit suffering humanity by making sick nursing an art in England. In the letter already quoted Miss Nightingale gives, in reply to a special appeal, advice to young women about their work: "1. I would say also to all young ladies who are called to any particular vocation, qualify yourselves for it, as a man does for his work. Don't think you can undertake it otherwise. No one should attempt to teach the Greek language until he is master of the language; and this he can only become by hard study. 2. If you are called to man's work, do not exact a woman's privileges—the privilege of inaccuracy, of weakness, ye muddleheads. Submit yourselves to the rules of business, as men do, by which alone you can make God's business succeed; for He has never said that He will give His success and His blessing to inefficiency, to sketchy and unfinished work."

Here, without intending it, Miss Nightingale drew a picture of her own character and methods. Years of hard study prepared her for her work; no inaccuracy, no weakness, no muddleheadedness was to be found in what she undertook; everything was business-like, orderly, and thorough. Those who knew her in the hospital spoke of her as combining "the voice of velvet and the will of steel." She was not content with having a natural vocation for her work. It is said that when she was a young girl she was accustomed to dress the wounds of those who were hurt in the lead mines and quarries of her Derbyshire home, and that the saying was, "Our good young miss is better than nurse or doctor." If this is accurate, she did not err by burying her talent in the earth, and thinking that because she had a natural gift there was no need to cultivate it. She saw rather that *because* she had a natural gift it was her duty to increase it and make it of the utmost benefit to mankind. At the end of her ten years' training, she came to the nursing home and hospital for governesses in Harley Street, an excellent institution, which at that time had fallen into some disorder through mismanagement. She stayed here from August 1853 till October 1854, and in those fourteen months placed the domestic, financial, and sanitary affairs of the little hospital on a sound footing.

Now, however, the work with which her name will always be associated, and for which she will always be loved and honoured, was about to commence. The Crimean war broke out early in 1854, and within a very few weeks of the commencement of actual fighting, every one at home was horrified and ashamed to hear of the frightful disorganisation of the supplies, and of the utter breakdown of the commissariat and medical arrangements. The most hopeless hugger-mugger reigned triumphant. The tinned meats sent out from England were little better than poison; ships arrived with stores of boots which proved all to be for the left foot. (Muddleheads do not all belong to one sex.) The medical arrangements for the sick and wounded were on a par with the rest. Mr. Justin M'Carthy, in his *History of Our Own Times*, speaks of the hospitals for the sick and wounded at Scutari as being in an absolutely chaotic condition. "In some instances," he writes, "medical stores were left to decay at Varna, or were found lying useless in the holds of vessels in Balaklava

Bay, which were needed for the wounded at Scutari. The medical officers were able and zealous men; the stores were provided and paid for so far as our Government was concerned; but the stores were not brought to the medical men. These had their hands all but idle, their eyes and souls tortured by the sight of sufferings which they were unable to relieve for want of the commonest appliances of the hospital" (vol. ii. p. 316). The result was that the most frightful mortality prevailed, not so much from the inevitable risks of battle, but from the insanitary conditions of the camp, the want of proper food, clothing, and fuel, and the wretched hospital arrangements. Mr. Mackenzie, author of a *History of the Nineteenth Century*, gives the following facts and figures with regard to our total losses in the Crimea: "Out of a total loss of 20,656, only 2598 were slain in battle; 18,058 died in hospital." "Several regiments became literally extinct. One had but seven men left fit for duty; another had thirty. When the sick were put on board transports, to be conveyed to hospital, the mortality was shocking. In some ships one man in every four died in a voyage of seven days. In some of the hospitals recovery was the rare exception. At one time four-fifths of the poor fellows who underwent amputation died of hospital gangrene. During the first seven months of the siege the men perished by disease at a rate which would have extinguished the entire force in little more than a year and a half" (p. 171). When these facts became known in England, the mingled grief, shame, and anger of the whole nation were unbounded. It was then that Mr. Sidney Herbert, who was Minister of War, appealed to Miss Nightingale to organise and take out with her a band of trained nurses. It is needless to say that she consented. She was armed with full authority to cut the swathes of red tape that had proved shrouds to so many of our soldiers. On the 21st of October 1854 Miss Nightingale, accompanied by forty-two other ladies, all trained nurses, set sail for the Crimea. They arrived at Constantinople on 4th November, the eve of Inkerman, which was fought on 5th November. Their first work, therefore, was to receive into the wards, which were already filled by 2300 men, the wounded from what proved the severest and fiercest engagement of the campaign. Miss Nightingale and her band of nurses proved fully equal to the charge they had undertaken. She, by a combination of inexorable firmness with unvarying gentleness, evolved order out of chaos. After her arrival, there were no more complaints of the inefficiency of the hospital arrangements for the army. The extraordinary way in which she spent herself and let herself be spent will never be forgotten. She has been known to stand for twenty hours at a stretch, in order to see the wounded provided with every means of easing their condition. Her attention was directed not only to nursing the sick and wounded, but to removing the causes which had made the camp and the hospitals so deadly to their inmates. The extent of the work of mere nursing may be estimated by the fact that a few months after her arrival ten thousand sick men were under her care, and the rows of beds in one hospital alone, the Barrack Hospital at Scutari, measured two miles and one-third in length, with an average distance between each bed of two feet six inches. Miss Nightingale's personal influence and authority over the men were immensely and deservedly strong. They knew she had left the comforts and refinements of a wealthy home to be of service to them. Her slight delicate form, her steady nerve, her kindly conciliating manner, and her absolute self-devotion, awoke a passion of chivalrous feeling on the part of the men she tended. Sometimes a soldier would refuse to submit to a painful but necessary operation until a few calm sentences of hers seemed at once to allay the storm, and the man would submit willingly to the ordeal he had to undergo. One soldier said, "Before she came here, there was such cursin' and swearing, and after that it was as holy as a church." Another said to Mr. Sidney Herbert, "She would speak to one and another, and nod and smile to many more; but she could not do it to all, you know—we lay there in hundreds—but we could kiss her shadow as it fell, and lay our heads on the pillow again, content." This incident, of the wounded soldier turning to kiss her shadow as it passed, has been woven into a beautiful poem by Longfellow. It is called "Santa Filomena." The fact that she had been born in, and had been named after, the city of Florence, may have suggested to the poet to turn her name into the language of the country of her birth.

Miss Nightingale suffered from an attack of hospital fever in the spring of 1855, but as soon as possible she returned to her laborious post, and never quitted it till the war was over and the last of our soldiers was on his way home. When she returned to England she received such a welcome as probably has fallen to no other woman; all distinctions of party and of rank were forgotten in the one wish to do her honour. She was presented by the Queen with a jewel in commemoration of her work in the Crimea, and a national testimonial was set on foot, to which a sum of £50,000 was subscribed. It is unnecessary to say that Miss Nightingale did not accept this testimonial for her own personal benefit. The sum was devoted to the permanent endowment of schools for the training of nurses in St. Thomas's and King's College Hospitals.

Since the Crimea no European war has taken place without calling forth the service of trained bands of skilled nurses. Within ten years of Florence Nightingale's labours in the East, the nations of Europe agreed at the Geneva Convention upon certain rules and regulations, with the object of ameliorating the condition of the sick and wounded in war. By this convention all ambulances and military hospitals were neutralised, and their inmates and staff were henceforth to be regarded as non-combatants. The distinguishing red cross of the Geneva Convention is now universally recognised as the one civilised element in the savagery of war.

During a great part of the years that have passed since Miss Nightingale returned from the Crimea, she has suffered from extremely bad health; but few people, even of the most robust frame, have done better and more invaluable work. She has been the adviser of successive Governments on the sanitary condition

63

of the army in India; her experience in the Crimea convinced her that the death-rate in the army, even in time of peace, could be reduced by nearly one-half by proper sanitary arrangements. She contributed valuable state papers on the subject to the Government of the day, and her advice has had important effects, not only on the condition of the army, but also on the sanitary reform of many of the towns of India, and on the extension of irrigation in that country. Besides this department of useful public work, she has written many books on the subjects she has made particularly her own; among them may be mentioned *Notes on Hospitals* and *Notes on Nursing*; the latter in particular is a book which no family ought to be without.

It will surprise no one to hear that she is very zealous for all that can lift up and improve the lives of women, and give them a higher conception of their duties and responsibilities. She supports the extension of parliamentary representation to women, generally, however, putting in a word in what she writes on the subject, to remind people that representatives will never be better than the people they represent. Therefore the most important thing for men, as well as for women, is to improve the education and morality of the elector, and then Parliament will improve itself. Every honest effort for the good of men or women has her sympathy, and a large number her generous support. May she long be spared to the country she has served so well, a living example of strength, courage, and self-forgetfulness—

A noble type of good
Heroic womanhood.

A Chapter from
Some Eminent Women of Our Times, 1889

RECOLLECTIONS OF FLORENCE NIGHTINGALE

By Linda Richards,
America's First Trained Nurse

In May, 1877, through the influence of Miss Nightingale, I was invited to visit St. Thomas Hospital Training School for as long a time as I wished. I went to the School and was made most welcome and comfortable for two months. I was given every advantage for observation in everything concerning the school and gained much valuable knowledge. I had been in the school only a few days when Miss Nightingale invited me to call upon her in her home. I went and was taken by the maid to Miss Nightingale's room — a large square room in which was a bed so placed that one could go around it without touching it. Upon the bed, dressed in black silk with a pretty lace cap upon her head, was Miss Nightingale. What I noticed particularly was her beautifully shaped head and her clear blue eyes which looked straight into mine. She extended a small delicate hand which gave mine a very friendly grasp; a chair was placed for me by the side of her bed, and for one hour we talked all about our own and English hospitals and training schools. While I was there a dainty lunch was served me. Miss Nightingale took particular interest in my work in London, and Edinburgh, advising me regarding the best hospitals to visit, and through her influence I was admitted to King's College Hospital as a visitor and also to the Royal Infirmary of Edinburgh. She invited me to visit her at her country home in Lee Hurst, where I spent several most enjoyable days, seeing Miss Nightingale some time each day and gaining much from her in every way. She questioned me carefully concerning our methods and the making of our young schools, and when I left her she said, "May you outstrip us that we may in turn outstrip you." To have had the honour of meeting Miss Nightingale I esteem as one of my greatest blessings.

A Chapter from
Reminiscences of Linda Richards, 1911

THE FLORENCE NIGHTINGALE MEDAL

An Article from
The British Journal of Nursing,
June 5th, 1920

The first awards of the Florence Nightingale Medal have now been made by the International Red Cross Committee at Geneva. The medal was instituted by the International Committee in 1912 in memory of the work of Miss Florence Nightingale, to be distributed annually to six trained nurses who, in the opinion of the Committee, have rendered exceptional service in connection with nursing. During the war no distribution was made, but shortly after the signing of peace it was decided to award fifty of these medals, and all National Red Cross Societies were requested to submit recommendations for consideration by the Committee. Forty-two medals have been awarded to the following :-

GREAT BRITAIN.

Mrs. John Lambert, of the Royal Naval Nursing
  Reserve, for services in 19 15 and 19 16, especially
  on the hospital ship *Rewa* at Gallipoli.
Miss Beatrice Isabel Jones, R.R.C., C.B.E., matron,
  Q.A.I.M.N.S., for services in Mesopotamia since 19 16.

Miss Gladys Laura White (Sister), B.R.C.S., for service,
1915 to 1918, especially at No. g B.R.C.S. Hospital
at St. Omer (No. 56 Casualty Clearing Station).

Miss Kate Maxey, R.R.C., M.M., (sister), T.F. Nursing
Service, for services from 1914 to 1918, .especially
at No. 58 Casualty Clearing Station.

Miss Gertrude Mary Wilton Smith, Q.A.1.M.N S,, for services
as sister-in-charge of Anglo-French hospital train No.
7 and No. 3 Casualty Clearing Station, France.

Miss Margaret Clotilde Macdonald, R.R.C., Matronin-
chief of the Canadian Army Nursing Service.

Miss Lucy Minchin, nursing sister of the British
Army in India and Mesopotamia.

Miss Hester Maclean, R.R.C., matron-in-chief,
New Zealand Army Nursing Service.

Mrs. E. R. Creagh, O.B.E., R.R.C., matron-in-chief,
South African Military Nursing Service.

AUSTRIA.

Mlle. Martha Paula Heller, Red Cross Hospital sister at Vienna;
employed on the Russian and Italian fronts and in Albania.

Mlle. Maria Adamczyk (Sister Theckla), Red Cross sister at
Vienna ; formerly served in the Balkan War, afterwards
head of the Red Cross Hospital at Lemburg.

BELGIUM.

Miss Astley Campbell, an English nurse, matron
of the Ocean Ambulance at Brussels.

Mlle. Kate Schandeleer, of the Edith Cave School.

DENMARK.

Mlle. Magdalene Tidemane, worked with the
   Danish Ambulances in France and with the
   American Red Cross at Belgrade.

UNITED STATES.

Miss Helen Scott Hay, of the North Western Academy, Illinois.
Miss Florence Merriam Johnson, trained at the New
   York Hospital Training School; a director of the
   nursing department of the Atlantic Division.
Miss Martha M. Russell, trained at the New York,
   Hospital Training School ; also with the
   Atlantic Division Department and matron of
   the University Hospital, Bidder, Colorado.
Miss Linda K. Meirs, trained at Philadelphia Hospital;
   served in Germany in 1914, France 1915, Rumania and
   elsewhere ; matron of the Naval Hospital at Boston.
Miss Alma E. Forster, trained at the Presbyterian Hospital,
   Chicago; served in Russia 1914, the American Red
   Cross in Rumania in 1917, and Russia 19 18.
Miss Mary E. Gladwin, trained at the Boston City Hospital
   ; served at Nisch in 1914, and 1917 to 1919.

FRANCE.

Mme. Marie Panas (*nee* Valli), of the Societe
   de Secours aux Blesses Militaires.
Mme. *veuve* Germaine le Grix (*nee* St. Girons),
   Association des Dames Francaises.
Mme. Louise Hugues (*nee* Leclerc), Union des Femmes
   de France, President of the Comite de St. Quentin.

69

Mlle Christine de Chevron de Vilette, Societe
de Secours aux Blesses Militaires.
Mme. la Marquise de Clapiers (*nee* de Foresta),
Societe Secours aux Blesses Militaires,
President of the Cornit6 de Marseilles.
Mlle. Marguerite Voisin, Societe de Secours
aux Blesses Militaires.
Mlle. Renee Aline Flourens, Union des Femmes de France.
Mlle. Marie Elisabeth Lajusan, Association
des Dames Francaises.

GREECE.

Mlle. Helene Vassiloboulo.

HUNGARY.

Baronne Eizella Apor,
Mlle. Ilona Durgo.

ITALY.

H.R.H. Elena di Francia, Duchessa D'Aosta,
Mlle. Ina Battistella,
Mlle. Maria Concetta Clhudzinska,
Mlle. Maria Andina,
Mlle. Maria Antonietta Clerigi.

JAPAN.

Mme. Take Hagiwara,

Mme. Ya-o Poinamoto,
Mme. Ume Yu-asa.

RUMANIA.

Mlle. Elenore Mihailescu.

CZECHO-SLOVAKIA.

Mlle. Irene Metekickova,
Mlle. Sylva Macharova.

Switzerland, not being among the belligerent nations, preferred not to put forward any names.

CLARA BARTON

1821 — 1912

CLARA BARTON
"THE ANGEL OF THE BATTLEFIELDS"

By Kate Dickinson Sweetser

For several weeks the sound of hammer and saw had been heard on the Barton farm where a new barn was being built. The framework was almost up, and David Barton and his little sister Clara, with a group of friends, were eagerly watching the carpenters, who were just fixing the high rafters to the ridge-pole.

"I dare you to climb to the top, Dave!" suddenly challenged a boy in the group.

David Barton, who was known as the "Buffalo Bill" of the neighbourhood, always took a dare. Almost before the challenge had been given his coat was off and he had started toward the new building amid a chorus of cries: "Good for you, Dave!" from the group of young spectators who were always thrilled by his daring exploits. Only the little sister Clara protested.

"Don't, David," she exclaimed. "It isn't safe."

Her warning was not heeded. Up went the sure-footed athlete until he had almost reached the topmost peak of the barn. Crash! a board gave way under his feet, and down to the ground he was hurled, landing on his back on a pile of heavy boards. Limp and lifeless he lay there, a strange contrast to the vigorous young man who had climbed up the building only a few moments earlier, and the accident seemed to paralyze the faculties of those who saw it happen. It was not the builders or the older persons present who spoke first, but small, dark-eyed, determined Clara, who idolized her brother.

"Get mother, and go for the doctor, quick!" she commanded, and in less time than it takes to tell it the entire Barton family had been summoned to the scene of the disaster, and a doctor was bending over the unconscious man.

Dorothy and Sally, the grown-up sisters, hastily obeyed the doctor's orders, and made a room in the farm-house ready for their injured brother, while Stephen Barton and one of the workmen carried him in as gently as possible and laid him on the bed which he was not to leave for many weary months. Examination proved that the injury was a serious one, and there was need of careful and continuous nursing. To the surprise of the whole family, who looked on eleven-year-old Clara, the youngest of them all, as still a baby, when Mrs. Barton made ready to take charge of the sick-room, she found a resolute little figure seated by the bedside, with determination to remain there showing on every line of her expressive face.

"Let me take care of him! I can do it—I want to. Please, oh, please!" pleaded Clara.

At first the coveted permission was denied her, for how could a girl so young take care of a dangerously injured man? But as the weary days and nights of watching wore away and it seemed as if there would be no end to them, from sheer exhaustion the older members of the family yielded their places temporarily to Clara. Then one day when the doctor came and found her in charge, the sick-room was so tidy and quiet, and the young nurse was so clear-minded and ready to obey his slightest order, that when she begged him to let her take care of her brother he gave his hearty permission, and Clara had won her way.

From that time on, through long months, she was the member of the family whose entire thought and care was centered in the invalid. David was very sick for such a long time that it seemed as if he could never rally, and his one great comfort was having Clara near him. Hour after hour, and day after day, she sat by his bedside, his thin hand clasped in her strong one, with the patience of a much older, wiser nurse. She practically shut herself up in that sick-room for two whole years, and it seemed as if there was nothing too hard for her to do well and quickly, if in any way it would make David more comfortable. Finally a new kind of bath was tried with success. David was cured, and Clara Barton had served her earliest apprenticeship as a nurse.

Let us look back and see what went into the making of an eleven-year-old child who would give two years of her life to a task like that.

On Christmas Day of the year 1821, Clarissa Harlowe, as she was named, or "Clara" Barton, as she was always called, was born in her father's home near the town of Oxford, Worcester County, Massachusetts. Her oldest sister Dorothy was seventeen at that time, and her oldest brother Stephen, fifteen, while David was thirteen and Sally ten years old; so it was a long time since there had been a baby in the family, and all were so delighted over the event that Clara Barton says in her *Recollections*, "I am told the family jubilation upon the occasion was so great that the entire dinner and tea sets had to be changed for the serving of the noble guests who gathered."

The house in which the Christmas child was born was a simple farm-house on a hill-top, and inside nearly everything was home-made, even the crib in which the baby was cradled. Outside, the flat flagstone in front of the door was marked by the hand tools of the father. Stephen Barton, or Captain Barton as he was called, was a man of marked military tastes, who had served under "Mad Anthony" Wayne in campaigns against the Indians. In his youngest daughter Clara he found a real comrade, and, perched on his knee, she early gained a passionate love of her country and a child's simple knowledge of its history through the thrilling tales he told her. In speaking of those days she says:

"I listened breathlessly to his war stories. Illustrations were called for, and we made battles and fought them. Every shade of military etiquette was regarded. Colonels, captains, and sergeants were given their proper place and rank. So with the political world; the President, Cabinet, and leading officers of the government were learned by heart, and nothing gratified the keen humour of my father more than the parrot-like readiness with which I lisped these difficult names." That they did not mean much even to such a precocious child as Clara Barton is shown by an incident of those early days, when her sister Dorothy asked her how she supposed a Vice-President looked.

"I suppose he is about as big as our barn, and green!" was the quick reply.

But though the child did not understand all that was poured into her greedy little mind by an eager father, yet it bore fruit in later years, for she says: "When later I ... was suddenly thrust into the mysteries of war, and had to take my place and part in it, I found myself far less a stranger to the conditions than most women, or even ordinary men, for that matter. I never addressed a colonel as captain, got my cavalry on foot, or mounted my infantry!"

When she was not listening to her father's stories or helping her mother with the housework, which, good housewife that Mrs. Barton was, she took great pains to teach her youngest daughter how to do well, Clara was as busy as possible in some other way. In that household there were no drones, and the little girl was not even allowed to waste time in playing with dolls, although she was given time to take care of her pets, of which she had an ever-increasing collection, including dogs, cats, geese, hens, turkeys, and even two heifers which she learned to milk.

Dorothy, Sally and Stephen Barton were teachers, and as Clara early showed her quick mentality, they all took great interest in educating her according to their different ideas. As a result, when the little girl was three years old she could read a story to herself, and knew a little bit about geography, arithmetic and spelling. That decided the family. Such a bright mind must be developed as early as possible. So on a fine, clear winter morning Stephen lifted her to his shoulders with a swing of his strong arms, and in that way she rode to the school taught by Col. Richard C. Stone, a mile and a half from the Barton farm. Although the new pupil was such a very little girl, and so shy that often she was not able even to answer when she was spoken to or to join the class in reciting Bible verses or in singing songs, yet Colonel Stone was deeply interested in her, and his manner of teaching was so unusual that the years with him made a lasting impression on his youngest scholar's mind. To Clara it was a real loss when, at the end of five years, the Colonel left the school, to be succeeded by Clara's sisters in summer and by her brother Stephen in winter.

David was Clara's favorite brother. So athletic was he, and so fond of all forms of out-of-door life and exercise, that he was no less than a hero to the little sister, who watched him with intense admiration, and in her secret heart determined that some day and in some way she, too, would be brave and daring.

Having decided this in her own mind, when David suggested teaching her to ride, she was delighted, and, hiding her fear, at once took her first lesson on one of the beautiful blooded colts which were a feature of her father's farm. In her *Story of My Childhood* she says: "It was David's delight to take me, a little girl five years old, to the field, seize a couple of those beautiful grazing creatures, broken only to the halter and bit, and, gathering the reins of both bridles in one hand, throw me on the back of one colt, spring on the other himself, and, catching me by the foot and bidding me 'cling fast to the mane,' gallop away over field and fen, in and out among the other colts, in wild glee like ourselves. They were merry rides we took. This was my riding-school. I never had any other, but it served me well.... Sometimes in later years when I found myself on a strange horse, in a troop saddle, flying for life or liberty in front of pursuit, I blessed the baby lessons of the wild gallops among the colts."

And so it was that the child grew strong in body and alert in mind, while the routine of daily farm duties, when she was not at school or galloping over the fields with David, developed her in concentration and in inventive ability. Housekeeping at that time was crude, and most of the necessary articles used were made at home. There were no matches. The flint snapped by the lock was the only way of lighting a fire. Garments were homespun, and home-made food was dried, canned and cooked in large quantities by the busy housekeeper. Although there was always a fire blazing on the hearth of the home, it was thought to be a religious duty to have the meeting-house unheated on the Sabbath day. Little Clara, who was particularly susceptible to cold, bore the bitter chill of the building as bravely as she could, each week in the long winter, but one Sunday as she sat in the big pew, not daring to swing her feet, they grew more and more numb until at last, when she was obliged to stand on them, she fell over—her poor little feet were frozen, and she had to be carried home and thawed out!

When she was eight years old her father left his hill farm and moved down to the Learned house, a much bigger farm of three hundred acres, with the brook-like French river winding through its broad meadows, and three great barns standing in the lowlands between the hill and the house. Stephen and David remained on the hill to work their small farms there, and the other sisters stayed there, but Clara was not lonesome in the new home in the valley, for at that time she had as playmates the four children of Captain Barton's nephew, who had recently died. With them Clara played hide-and-seek in the big hay-mows, and other interesting games. Her most marked characteristic then and for many years afterward was her excessive shyness, yet when there was anything to do which did not include conversation she was always the champion. At times she was so bashful that even speaking to an intimate friend was often an agony to her, and it is said she once stayed home from meeting on Sunday rather than tell her mother that her gloves were too worn out to wear!

Inside the new house she found many fascinating things to do, and did them with eager interest. The house was being redecorated, and Clara went from room to room, watching the workmen, and even learned to grind and mix paints. Then she turned her attention to the paperers, who were so much amused with the child's cleverness that they showed her how to match, trim and hang paper, and in every room they good-naturedly let her paste up some piece of the decoration, so she felt that the house was truly hers, and never lost her affection for it in any of her later wanderings or changes of residence.

When the new home was completed inside Clara turned her attention to out-of-door matters and found more than one opportunity for daring feats. With shining eyes and bated breath, she learned to cross the little winding French river on teetering logs at its most dangerous depths. When this grew tame, she would go to the sawmill and ride out on the saw carriage twenty feet above the stream, and be pulled back on the returning log, and oh the joy of such dangerous sport!

By the time she was eleven years old her brothers had been so successful with their hill farms that they followed their father down to the valley of the river, where they bought the sawmill and built new dams and a grain-mill, and Sally and Stephen, who both married, settled in homes near the Barton farm. Then came the building of the new barn and David's accident. Eleven-year-old Clara, a child in years but mature mentally, proved equal to the emergency and took up her role of nurse in the same vigorous way she went about everything—but she had to pay a high price for her devotion.

David was strong and well again, but the little sister who had been his constant companion through the weary months was far from normal. The family had been so occupied with the invalid that no thought had been given to his young nurse. Now with grave concern Captain Barton talked with his wife.

"She has not gained an ounce in weight in these two years," he said, "and she isn't an inch taller. If anything, she seems to be more morbidly self-conscious and shy than ever. What shall we do with her?"

That was the question. The years shut up in the sick-room had completely unfitted Clara for ordinary life; she seemed to be more afraid of speaking to any one, more afraid of being seen or talked to than ever before. All took a hand at helping her to forget herself. Sally, who knew what an imaginative nature her small sister had, interested her in reading poetry, which was a delight to Clara. At the same time her father and brothers kept her out-of-doors as much as possible, and her father gave her a fine horse of her own. She named him Billy, and at once jumped on his back to get acquainted. From that time the slim, graceful animal with his youthful rider became one of the features of the neighbourhood as they galloped across country. But, despite all that was done to make her healthy and happy, her self-consciousness and shyness remained, and another way of curing her was tried. She was sent to the boarding-school which was kept by her old teacher, Colonel Stone. He was delighted to have her in the school, and her quick mind was an amazement to him; but she was so homesick that often it was impossible for her to study or to recite, while being with one hundred and fifty girls of her own age made her more bashful than ever. In despair, Colonel Stone advised her father to take her home before she became seriously sick, and soon she found herself again in her beloved haunts. After that time her brother Stephen taught her mathematics; and later, when two fine teachers came to Oxford, she studied Latin, philosophy and chemistry with them, besides literature, history and languages—finding herself far ahead of the other scholars of her age, although she had been buried in a sick-room for two years.

As long as she was busy she was contented, but when vacation came she was again miserable. Her active mind and body demanded constant work; when she did not have it she was simply wretched, and made those around her so.

One day, when she was in her brother's mill watching the busy weavers, she had a sudden desire to work a loom herself. When she mentioned this at home her mother was horrified, but Stephen, who understood her restless nature better, took Clara's side and a few days later she proudly took her place before her loom and with enthusiastic persistence mastered the mysteries of the flying shuttle. How long she would have kept on with the work cannot be guessed, for on the fifteenth day after she began work the mill burned down, and she was again on the look-out for new employment for her active brain and body.

That she was a real girl was shown when, having discovered that she had no summer hat, she decided she must have one. Walking through the rye-fields, she had an idea. With quick interest in a new accomplishment, she cut a number of green rye stalks, carried them into the house and scalded them, then laid them out in the sun to bleach, and when they were white, she cut them into even lengths, pulled them apart with her teeth, braided them in eleven strands and made the first straw bonnet she ever owned.

Somehow or other the months of vacation wore away; then the question was, what to do next? Her nature demanded constant action. She was far ahead of others of her own age in the matter of studies, and Mrs. Barton was in real bewilderment as to what to do with her youngest child. A phrenologist, who was a keen observer of child nature, was visiting the Bartons at that time, and Clara, who had the mumps and was lying on the lounge in the adjoining room, heard her mother tell their guest of her daughter's restlessness and self-consciousness and ask his advice. Listening eagerly, she heard his reply:

"The sensitive nature will always remain," he said. "She will never assert herself for herself; she will suffer wrong first. But for others she will be perfectly fearless. Throw responsibility upon her. Give her a school to teach."

The very words, "give her a school to teach," sent a shiver of fear through Clara's frame, as she lay there listening, but at the same time she felt a thrill of pleasure at the idea of doing something so important as teaching. If her mother was so much troubled about her peculiar traits as to be obliged to talk them over with a stranger, they must be very hard to bear. She would set to work to be something quite different, and she would begin at once!

And so it happened that when Clara Barton was fifteen years old she followed in the footsteps of her brother and sisters and became a teacher. As soon as she decided to take the step, she was given District School No. 9, up in "Texas village," and in May, 1836, "after passing the teachers' examination with a mark of 'excellent,' she put down her skirts and put up her hair and walked to the little schoolhouse, to face and address her forty scholars." That was one of the most awful moments of her life. When the rows of pupils were ranged before her, and she was supposed to open the exercises by reading from the Bible, she could not find her voice, and her hand trembled so visibly that she was afraid to turn the pages and so disclose her panic. But no one knew. With perfect outward calmness, she kept her eyes on the open book until her pulse beat less fast, then she looked straight ahead and in a steady voice asked them to each read a verse in turn. This was a new and delightful plan to her pupils, who were still more pleased when the reading was over to have the new teacher question them in a friendly way about the meaning of the verses they had just read in the "Sermon on the Mount."

That first day proved her marked ability as a teacher, and so kindly and intimate was she with her scholars that they became more her comrades than her pupils. When the four rough boys of the school "tried her out" to see how much she could endure, to their astonishment, instead of being able to lock her out of the building as they had done with the previous teacher, she showed such pluck and physical strength that their respect was won and kept. After that, almost daily, at recess time she would join them in games such as no teacher had ever played with them before. And with her success Clara gained a new assurance and a less shy manner, although she never entirely lost her self-consciousness.

So successful was she with that first school that it was the preface to sixteen years of continuous teaching, winter and summer. Her two most interesting experiences as a teacher were in North Oxford and in Bordentown, New Jersey. North Oxford was the mill village where her brother's factories were, and where there were hundreds of children. When her popularity as the teacher in No. 9, Texas village, spread to North Oxford, she was asked to go there to start a school for operatives. This was a piece of work to her liking, and for ten years she says: "I stood with them in the crowded school-room summer and winter, without change or relaxation. I saw my little lisping boys become overseers, and my stalwart overseers become business men and themselves owners of mills. My little girls grew to be teachers and mothers of families." Here was satisfying work for the busy brain and active body! But even that did not take up all of her time; she found long hours in which to read and study, and also acted as Stephen's bookkeeper in the mill, during those years in North Oxford.

At the end of the ten years she broke away from the routine of teaching and became a pupil herself in Clinton Liberal Institute in New York, as there were no colleges for women at that time. The year of study refreshed her in mind and body, and, as her mother died during the year and her father decided to live with his married children, Clara was free to seek the work of the world wherever it should claim her.

From the seminary she went to Hightstown to teach, and while there rumors of her ability to cope with conditions and unruly scholars reached the village of Bordentown, ten miles away from Hightstown. Many attempts had been made to start a public school there, but without success. As a result the children of the poor ran wild in the streets, or when an attempt was made to open a school they broke up the sessions by their lawless behavior. When she heard this, Clara Barton was so greatly interested that she went to Bordentown to talk it over with the town officials, who told her that it was useless to think of making the experiment again.

Clara Barton's eyes flashed with determination. "Give me three months, and I will teach free!" she said.

As a result of her generous offer, she was allowed to rent a tumble-down, unoccupied building, and opened her school with six pupils! Every one of the six became so enthusiastic over a teacher who was interested in each individual that their friends were eager to be her pupils, too, and parents were anxious to see what the wonderful little bright-eyed, friendly woman could do for their children. At the end of five weeks the building was too small for her scholars, and the roll-call had almost six hundred names on it. To a triumphant teacher who had volunteered her services to try an experiment, a regular salary was now offered and an assistant given her. And so Clara Barton again proved her talent for teaching.

But Bordentown was her last school. When she had been there for two years and perfected the public-school system, her voice gave out as a result of constant use, and she went to Washington for a rest. But it did not take her long to recuperate, and soon she was eagerly looking out for some new avenue of opportunity to take the place of teaching. Government work interested her, and she heard rumors of scandals in the Patent Office, where some dishonest clerks had been copying and selling the ideas of inventors who had filed patents. This roused her anger, for she felt the inventors were defrauded and undefended individuals who needed a protector. As her brother's bookkeeper, she had developed a clear, copper-plate handwriting, which would aid her in trying to get the position she determined to try for. Through a relative in Congress she secured a position in the Patent Office, and when it was proved that she was acceptable there, although she was the first woman ever appointed independently to a clerkship in the department, she was given charge of a confidential desk, where she had the care of such papers as had not been carefully enough guarded before. Her salary of $1,400 a year was as much as was received by the men in the department, which created much jealousy, and she had many sneers and snubs and much disagreeable treatment from the other clerks; but she went serenely on her way, doing her duty and enjoying the new line of work with its chances for observation of the government and its working.

War clouds were now beginning to gather over both North and South, and signs of an approaching conflict were ominously clear in Washington, where slavery sentiments swayed all departments. Clara Barton saw with keen mental vision all the signs of the times, and there was much to worry her, for from the first she was clearly and uncompromisingly on the unpopular side of the disturbing question, and believed with Charles Sumner that "Freedom is national; slavery is sectional." She believed in the Union and she believed in the freedom of the individual. So eager was she to help the government in the coming national crisis that she offered her services as a clerk, to do the work of two dishonest men; for this work she was to receive the salary of one clerk, and pay back into the Treasury that of the other, in order to save all the money possible for an emergency. No deed gives a clearer insight into the character of Clara Barton than that. As it was in the case of the school in Bordentown, so was it now. If public service was the question, she had no thought of self or of money—the point was to achieve the desired end. And now she was nearer the goal of her own personal service to the world than she dreamed.

Fort Sumter was fired on. President Lincoln called for seventy-five thousand troops, and all those who were at the seat of government knew that the hour for sacrifice of men and money had come. Massachusetts responded to the call for troops with four regiments, one of which, the Sixth, set out for Washington at once. As they marched through the streets of Baltimore they were attacked by a furious mob who succeeded in killing four soldiers and wounding many more, but the troopers fought them off as bravely as possible and marched on to the station, where they entrained for Washington, many of them arriving there in a pitiable condition. When they detrained at the national capital they were met by a large number of sympathetic women, among them Clara Barton, who recognized some of her old friends and pupils among those who were limping, or with injured arms, or carried on stretchers, and her heart went out to them in loyalty and pride, for they were giving their services to their country in an hour of need.

The men who had not been injured were temporarily quartered at the Capitol, while the wounded were taken to the Infirmary, where their wounds were dressed at once, any material on hand being used. When the supply of handkerchiefs gave out, Clara Barton, as well as other impromptu nurses, rushed to their homes and tore up sheets for bandages, and Miss Barton also filled a large box full of needles, pins, buttons, salves and other necessities, and carried it back to the Infirmary, where she had her first experience in caring for wounded soldiers. When she could leave the Infirmary, she went to the Capitol and found the poor fellows there famished, for they had not been expected and their commissary stores had not yet been unloaded. Down to the market hurried the energetic volunteer nurse, and soon came back carrying a big basketful of supplies, which made a feast for the hungry men. Then, as she afterward wrote in a letter to a friend, "the boys, who had just one copy of the *Worcester Spy* of the 22nd, were so anxious to know its contents that they begged me to read it to them, which I did—mounting to the desk of the President of the Senate, that they all might hear."

In her letter she says, "You would have smiled to see *me* and my *audience* in the Senate Chamber of the U. S. A." and adds: "God bless the noble fellows who leave their quiet happy homes at the call of their country. So far as our poor efforts can reach, they shall never lack a kindly hand or a sister's sympathy if they come."

Eager to have the soldiers given all the comforts and necessities which could be obtained, Miss Barton put an advertisement in the *Worcester Spy*, asking for supplies and money for the wounded and needy in the Sixth Regiment, and stating that she herself would receive and give them out. The response was overwhelming. So much food and clothing was sent to her that her small apartment overflowed with supplies, and she was obliged to rent rooms in a warehouse to store them.

And now Clara Barton was a new creature. She felt within herself the ability to meet a great need, and the energy which for so long had been pent up within her was poured out in a seemingly unending supply of tenderness and of help for suffering humanity. There was no time now for sensitiveness, or for shyness; there was work to do through the all-too-short days and nights of this struggle for freedom and unity of the nation. Gone was the teacher, gone the woman of normal thought and action, and in her place we find the "Angel of the Battlefields," who for the remainder of her life was to be one of the world's foremost figures in ministrations to the suffering, where suffering would otherwise have had no alleviation.

"On the 21st of July the Union forces were routed at Bull Run with terrific loss of life and many wounded. Two months later the battle of Ball's Bluff occurred, in which there were three Massachusetts regiments engaged, with many of Clara Barton's lifelong friends among them. By this time the hospitals and commissaries in Washington had been well organized, and there was no desperate need for the supplies which were still being shipped to Miss Barton in great quantities, nor was there need of her nursing. However, she went to the docks to meet the wounded and dying soldiers, who were brought up the Potomac on transports." Often they were in such a condition from neglect that they were baked as hard as the backs of turtles with blood and clay, and it took all a woman's swift and tender care, together with the use of warm water, restoratives, dressings, and delicacies to make them at all comfortable. Then their volunteer nurse would go with them to the hospitals, and back again in the ambulance she would drive, to repeat her works of mercy.

But she was not satisfied with this work. If wounds could be attended to as soon as the men fell in battle, hundreds of deaths could be prevented, and she made up her mind that in some way she was going to override public sentiment, which in those early days of the war did not allow women nurses to go to the front, for she was determined to go to the very firing-line itself as a nurse. And, as she had got her way at other times in her life, so now she achieved her end, but after months of rebuffs and of tedious waiting, during which the bloody battle of Fair Oaks had been fought with terrible losses on each side. The seven days' retreat of the Union forces under McClellan followed, with eight thousand wounded and over seventeen hundred killed. On top of this came the battle of Cedar Mountain, with many Northerners killed, wounded and missing.

One day, when Assistant Quartermaster-General Rucker, who was one of the great-hearts of the army, was at his desk, he was confronted by a bright-eyed little woman, to whose appeal he gave sympathetic attention.

"I have no fear of the battle-field," she told him. "I have large stores, but no way to reach the troops."

Then she described the condition of the soldiers when they reached Washington, often too late for any care to save them or heal their wounds. She *must* go to the battle-front where she could care for them quickly. So overjoyed was she to be given the needed passports as well as kindly interest and good wishes that she burst into tears as she gripped the old soldier's hand, then she hurried out to make immediate plans for having her supplies loaded on a railroad car. As she tersely put it, "When our armies fought on Cedar Mountain, I broke the shackles and went to the field." When she began her work on the day after the battle she found an immense amount of work to do. Later she described her experience in this modest way:

"Five days and nights with three hours' sleep—a narrow escape from capture—and some days of getting the wounded into hospitals at Washington brought Saturday, August 30th. And if you chance to feel that the positions I occupied were rough and unseemly for a woman, I can only reply that they were rough and unseemly for men. But under all, lay the life of a nation. I had inherited the rich blessing of health and strength of constitution such as are seldom given to women, and I felt that some return was due from me and that I ought to be there."

The famous army nurse had served her novitiate now, and through the weary years of the war which dragged on with alternate gains and losses for the Union forces, Clara Barton's name began to be spoken of with awe and deep affection wherever a wounded man had come under her gentle care. Being under no society or leader, she was free to come or go at will. But from the first day of her work at the front she was encouraged in it by individual officers who saw the great value of what she accomplished.

At Antietam, when the fighting began, her wagons were driven through a field of tall corn to an old homestead, while the shot whizzed thick around them. In the barnyard and among the corn lay torn and bleeding men—the worst cases, just brought from the places where they had fallen. All was in confusion, for the army medical supplies had not yet arrived, and the surgeons were trying to make bandages of corn husks. The new army nurse immediately had her supplies unloaded and hurried out to revive the wounded with bread soaked in wine. When her bread gave out there were still many to be fed. All the supplies she had were three cases of unopened wine.

"Open the wine, and give that," she commanded, "and God help us."

Her order was obeyed, and as she watched the cases being unpacked her eyes fell on the packing around the bottles of wine. It was nicely sifted corn-meal. If it had been gold dust it could not have been more valuable. The wine was unpacked as quickly as possible; kettles were found in the farm-house, and in a twinkling that corn-meal was mixed with water, and good gruel for the men was in the making. Then it occurred to Miss Barton to see what was in the cellar of the old house, and there three barrels of flour and a bag of salt were found, stored by the rebels and left behind when they marched away. "What wealth!" exclaimed the woman, who was frantically eager to feed her flock. All that night Clara Barton and her workers carried buckets of hot gruel up and down the long lines to the wounded and dying men. Then up to the farm-house went the army nurse, where, in the dim light of a lone flickering candle, she could dimly see the surgeon in charge, sitting in apparent despair by the table, his head resting in his hands. She tiptoed up to him and said, quietly, "You are tired, doctor."

Looking up, he exclaimed: "Tired? Yes, I am tired! Tired of such heartlessness and carelessness! And," he added, "think of the condition of things. Here are at least one thousand wounded men; terribly wounded, five hundred of whom cannot live till daylight without attention. That two-inch of candle is all I have, or can get. What can I do? How can I bear it?"

A smile played over Clara Barton's clear-cut face. Gently but firmly she took him by the elbow and led him to the door, pointing toward the barn, where dozens of lanterns gleamed like stars.

"What is it?" he exclaimed.

"The barn is lighted," she said, "and the house will be directly."

"Who did it?"

"I, doctor."

"Where did you get them?"

"Brought them with me."

"How many have you?"

"All you want, four boxes."

For a moment he stared at her as if to be sure he was not in a dream. Then he turned away without a word, and never spoke of the matter again, but his deference to Clara Barton from that time was the greatest a man can pay a woman.

Not until all her stores were exhausted and she was sick with a fever would Clara Barton leave the battle-field of Antietam; then, dragging herself to the train, she went back to Washington to be taken care of until she was better. When at last she was strong enough to work again she went to see her friend Quartermaster-General Rucker, and told him that if she had had five wagons she would have had enough supplies for all the wounded at Antietam. With an expression of intense admiration on his soldierly face as he watched the brave volunteer nurse, he declared:

"You shall have enough next time!"

The promise was made good. Having recognized the value of her efficient services, the Government assisted in every way, making it possible for her to carry on her work on the battle-fields and in military camps and hospitals in the best way.

Clara Barton!—Only the men who lay wounded or dying on the battle-field knew the thrill and the comfort that the name carried. Again and again her life was in danger—once at Antietam, when stooping to give a drink of water to an injured boy, a bullet whizzed between them. It ended the life of the poor lad, but only tore a hole in Clara Barton's sleeve. And so, again and again, it seemed as if a special Providence protected her from death or injury. At Fredericksburg, when the dead, starving and wounded lay frozen on the ground, and there was no effective organization for proper relief, with swift, silent efficiency Clara Barton moved among them, having the snow cleared away and under the banks finding famished, frozen figures which were once men. She rushed to have an old chimney torn down and built fire-blocks, over which she soon had kettles full of coffee and gruel steaming.

As she was bending over a wounded rebel, he whispered to her: "Lady, you have been kind to me ... every street of the city is covered by our cannon. When your entire army has reached the other side of the Rappahannock, they will find Fredericksburg only a slaughter-pen. Not a regiment will escape. Do not go over, for you will go to certain death."

She thanked him for the kindly warning and later told of the call that came to her to go across the river, and what happened. She says:

"At ten o'clock of the battle day when the rebel fire was hottest, the shells rolling down every street, and the bridge under the heavy cannonade, a courier dashed over, and, rushing up the steps of the house where I was, placed in my hand a crumpled, bloody piece of paper, a request from the lion-hearted old surgeon on the opposite shore, establishing his hospitals in the very jaws of death:

"'Come to me,' he wrote. 'Your place is here.'

"The faces of the rough men working at my side, which eight weeks before had flushed with indignation at the thought of being controlled by a woman, grew ashy white as they guessed the nature of the summons, ... and they begged me to send them, but save myself. I could only allow them to go with me if they chose, and in twenty minutes we were rocking across the swaying bridge, the water hissing with shot on either side.

"Over into that city of death, its roofs riddled by shell, its every church a crowded hospital, every street a battle-line, every hill a rampart, every rock a fortress, and every stone wall a blazing line of forts.

"Oh, what a day's work was that! How those long lines of blue, rank on rank, charged over the open acres, up to the very mouths of those blazing guns, and how like grain before the sickle they fell and melted away.

"An officer stepped to my side to assist me over the débris at the end of the bridge. While our hands were raised in the act of stepping down, a piece of an exploding shell hissed through between us, just below our arms, carrying away a portion of both the skirts of his coat and my dress, rolling along the ground a few rods from us like a harmless pebble in the water. The next instant a solid shot thundered over our heads, a noble steed bounded in the air and with his gallant rider rolled in the dirt not thirty feet in the rear. Leaving the kind-hearted officer, I passed on alone to the hospital. In less than a half-hour he was brought to me—dead."

She was passing along a street in the heart of the city when she had to step aside to let a regiment of infantry march by. At that moment General Patrick saw her, and, thinking she was a frightened resident of the city who had been left behind in the general exodus, leaned from his saddle and said, reassuringly:

"You are alone and in great danger, madam. Do you want protection?"

With a rare smile, Miss Barton said, as she looked at the ranks of soldiers, "Thank you, but I think I am the best-protected woman in the United States."

The near-by soldiers caught her words and cried out:

"That's so! That's so!" and the cheer they gave was echoed by line after line, until the sound of the shouting was like the cheers after a great victory. Bending low with a courtly smile, the general said:

"I believe you are right, madam!" and galloped away.

"At the battles of Cedar Mountain, Second Bull Run, Antietam, during the eight months' siege of Charleston, in the hospital at Fort Wagner, with the army in front of Petersburg and in the Wilderness and the hospitals about Richmond, there was no limit to the work Clara Barton accomplished for the sick and dying, but among all her experiences during those years of the war, the Battle of Fredericksburg was most unspeakably awful to her. And yet afterward she saw clearly that it was this defeat that gave birth to the Emancipation Proclamation.

"And the white May blossoms of '63 fell over the glad faces— the swarthy brows, the toil-worn hands of four million liberated slaves. 'America,' writes Miss Barton, 'had freed a race.'"

As the war drew to an end, President Lincoln received hundreds of letters from anxious parents asking for news of their boys. There were eighty thousand missing men whose families had no knowledge whether they were alive or dead. In despair, and believing that Clara Barton had more information of the soldiers than any one else to whom he could turn, the President requested her to take up the task, and the army nurse's tender heart was touched by the thought of helping so many mothers who had no news of their boys, and she went to work, aided by the hospital and burial lists she had compiled when on the field of action.

For four years she did this work, and it was a touching scene when she was called before the Committee on Investigation to tell of its results. With quiet simplicity she stood before the row of men and reported, "Over thirty thousand men, living and dead, already traced. No available funds for the necessary investigation; in consequence, over eight thousand dollars of my own income spent in the search."

As the men confronting her heard the words of the bright-eyed woman who was looked on as a sister by the soldiers from Maine to Virginia, whose name was a household one throughout the land, not one of them was ashamed to wipe the tears from his eyes! Later the government paid her back in part the money she had spent in her work; but she gave her time without charge as well as many a dollar which was never returned, counting it enough reward to read the joyful letters from happy, reunited families.

While doing this work she gave over three hundred lectures through the East and West, and as a speaker she held her audiences as if by magic, for she spoke glowingly about the work nearest to her heart, giving the proceeds of her lectures to the continuance of that work. One evening in the winter of 1868, when speaking in one of the finest opera-houses in the East, before one of the most brilliant assemblages she had ever faced, her voice suddenly gave out, as it had in the days when she was teaching. The heroic army nurse and worker for the soldiers was worn out in body and nerves. As soon as she was able to travel the doctor commanded that she take three years of absolute rest. Obeying the order, she sailed for Europe, and in peaceful Switzerland with its natural beauty hoped to regain normal strength; for her own country had emerged from the black shadow of war, and she felt that her life work had been accomplished, that rest could henceforth be her portion.

But Clara Barton was still on the threshold of her complete achievement. When she had been in Switzerland only a month, and her broken-down nerves were just beginning to respond to the change of air and scene, she received a call which changed the color of her future. Her caller represented the International Committee of the Red Cross Society. Miss Barton did not know what the Red Cross was, and said so. He then explained the nature of the society, which was founded for the relief of sick and wounded soldiers, and he told his eager listener what she did not know, that back of the Society was the Geneva Treaty, which had been providing for such relief work, signed by all the civilized nations except her own. From that moment a new ambition was born in Clara Barton's heart—to find out why America had not signed the treaty, and to know more about the Red Cross Society.

Nearly a year later, while still resting in quiet Switzerland, there broke one day upon the clear air of her Swiss home the distant sounds of a royal party hastening back from a tour of the Alps. To Miss Barton's amazement it came in the direction of her villa. Finally flashed the scarlet and gold of the liveries of the Grand Duke of Baden. After the outriders came the splendid coach of the Grand Duchess, daughter of King Wilhelm of Prussia, so soon to be Emperor William of Germany. In it rode the Grand Duchess. After presenting her card through the footman, she herself alighted and clasped Miss Barton's hand, hailing her in the name of humanity, and said she already knew her through what she had done in the Civil War. Then, still clasping her hand in a tight grip of comradeship, she begged Miss Barton to leave Switzerland and aid in Red Cross work on the battle-fields of the Franco-Prussian War, which was in its beginnings. It was a real temptation to once again work for suffering humanity, yet she put it aside as unwise. But a year later, when the officers of the International Red Cross Society came again to beg that Miss Barton take the lead in a great systematic plan of relief work such as that for which she had become famous during the Civil War, she accepted. In the face of such consequences as her health might suffer from her decision, she rose, and, with head held high and flashing eyes, said:

"Command me!"

Clara Barton was no longer to be the Angel of the American battle-fields only—from that moment she belonged to the world, and never again could she be claimed by any one country. But it is as the guardian angel of our soldiers in the United States that her story concerns us, although there is reason for great pride in the part she played in nursing the wounded at Strassburg, and later when her presence carried comfort and healing to the victims of the fight with the Commune in Paris.

As tangible results of her work abroad, she was given an amethyst cut in the shape of a pansy, by the Grand Duchess of Baden, also the Serbian decoration of the Red Cross as the gift of Queen Natalie, and the Gold Cross of Remembrance, which was presented her by the Grand Duke and Duchess of Baden together. Queen Victoria, with her own hand, pinned an English decoration on her dress. The Iron Cross of Germany, as well as the Order of Melusine given her by the Prince of Jerusalem, were among an array of medals and pendants—enough to have made her a much bejewelled person, had it been her way to make a show of her own rewards.

Truly Clara Barton belonged to the world, and a suffering person had no race or creed to her—she loved and cared for all.

When at last she returned to America, it was with the determination to have America sign the Geneva Treaty and to bring her own country into line with the Red Cross movement, which she had carefully watched in foreign countries, and which she saw was the solution to efficient aid of wounded men, either in the battle-field or wherever there had been any kind of disaster and there was need of quick aid for suffering. It was no easy task to convince American officials, but at last she achieved her end. On the 1st of March, 1882, the Geneva Treaty was signed by President Arthur, ratified by the Senate, and immediately the American National Red Cross was formed with Clara Barton as its first president.

The European "rest" trip had resulted in one of the greatest achievements for the benefit of mankind in which America ever participated, and its birth in the United States was due solely to the efforts of the determined, consecrated nurse who, when eleven years old, gave her all to a sick brother, and later consecrated her life to the service of a sick brotherhood of brave men.

On the day after her death, on April 12, 1912, one editor of an American newspaper paid a tribute to her that ranks with those paid the world's greatest heroes. He said:

"On the battle-fields of the Rebellion her hands bound up the wounds of the injured brave.

"The candles of her charity lighted the gloom of death for the heroes of Antietam and Fredericksburg.

"Across the ocean waters of her sweet labors followed the flag of the saintly Red Cross through the Franco-Prussian war.

"When stricken Armenia cried out for help in 1896, it was Clara Barton who led the relief corps of salvation and sustenance.

"A woman leading in answering the responsibility of civilization to the world!

"When McKinley's khaki boys struck the iron from Cuba's bondage it was Clara Barton, in her seventy-seventh year, who followed to the fever-ridden tropics to lead in the relief-work on Spanish battle-grounds.

"She is known wherever man appreciates humanity."

Hers was the honor of being the first president of the American Red Cross, but she was more than that—she *was* the Red Cross at that time. It was, as she said, "her child," and she furnished headquarters for it in her Washington home, dispensing the charities of a nation, amounting to hundreds of thousands of dollars, and was never requested to publish her accounts, an example of personal leadership which is unparalleled.

In 1897 we find the Red Cross president settled in her home at Glen Echo, a few miles out of Washington, on a high slope overlooking the Potomac, and, although it was a Red Cross center, it was a friendly lodging as well, where its owner could receive her personal friends. Flags and Red Cross testimonials from rulers of all nations fluttered from the walls, among them a beautiful one from the Sultan of Turkey. Two small crosses of red glass gleamed in the front windows over the balcony, but above the house the Red Cross banner floated high, as if to tell the world that "the banner over us is love." And to Glen Echo, the center of her beloved activity, Clara Barton always loved to return at the end of her campaigns. To the many thousands who came to visit her home as one of the great humane centers of the world, she became known as the "Beautiful Lady of the Potomac," and never did a title more fittingly describe a nature.

To the last she was a soldier—systematic, industrious, severely simple in her tastes. It was a rule of the household that every day's duties should be disposed of before turning in for the night, and at five o'clock the next morning she would be rolling a carpet-sweeper over the floor. She always observed military order and took a soldier's pride in keeping her quarters straight.

Hanging on the wall between her bedroom and private sitting-room was a small mirror into which her mother looked when she came home as a bride.

Her bed was small and hard. Near it were the books that meant so much to her—the Bible, Pilgrim's Progress, the stories of Sarah Orne Jewett, the poems of Lucy Larcom, and many other well-worn, much-read classics.

That she was still feminine, as in the days of girlhood when she fashioned her first straw bonnet, so now she was fond of wearing handsome gowns, often with trains. Lavender, royal purple, and wine color were the shades she liked best to wear, and in which her friends most often remember her. Despite her few extravagant tastes, Clara Barton was the most democratic woman America ever produced, as well as the most humane. She loved people, sick and well, and in any State and city of the Union she could claim personal friends in every walk of life.

When, after ninety-nine years of life and fifty of continuous service to suffering human nature, death laid its hand upon her on that spring day, the world to its remotest corner stopped its busy barter and trade for a brief moment to pay reverent tribute to a woman, who was by nature of the most retiring, bashful disposition, and yet carried on her life-work in the face of the enemy, to the sound of cannon, and close to the firing-line. She was on the firing-line all her life. That is her life story.

Her "boys" of all ages adored her, and no more touching incident is told of her than that of a day in Boston, when, after a meeting, she lingered at its close to chat with General Shafter. Suddenly the great audience, composed entirely of old soldiers, rose to their feet as she came down the aisle, and a voice cried:

"Three cheers for Clara Barton!"

They were given by voices hoarse with feeling. Then some one shouted:

"Tiger!"

Before it could be given another voice cried:

"No! *Sweetheart!*"

Then those grizzled elderly men whose lives she had helped to save broke into uproar and tears together, while the little bent woman smiled back at them with a love as true as any sweetheart's.

To-day we stand at the parting of the ways. Our nation is in the making as a world power, and in its rebirth there must needs be bloodshed and scalding tears. As we American girls and women go out bravely to face the untried future and to nurse under the banner of the Red Cross, we shall do our best work when we bear to the battle-field the same spirit of high purpose and consecration that inspired Clara Barton and made her the "Angel of the Battle-fields." Let us, as loyal Americans, take to heart part of a speech she once made on Memorial Day, when she stood with the "Boys in Blue" in the "God's-acre" of the soldier, and declared:

"We cannot always hold our great ship of state out of the storms and breakers. She must meet and buffet with them. Her timbers must creak in the gale. The waves must wash over her decks, she must lie in the trough of the sea as she does to-day. But the Stars and Stripes are above her. She is freighted with the hopes of the world. God holds the helm, and she's coming to port. The weak must fear, the timid tremble, but the brave and stout of heart will work and hope and trust."

A CHAPTER FROM
Ten American Girls from History, 1917

SERVICES IN TIME OF WAR.

By Clara Barton

Notwithstanding the readiness with which most persons will perceive the beneficent uses of relief societies in war, it may not be amiss to particularize some of the work accomplished by the societies of the Red Cross. Not to mention civil disturbances and lesser conflicts, they participated in not less than five great wars in the first ten years, commencing with Schleswig-Holstein, and ending with the Franco-German. Russia and Turkey have followed, with many others since that time, in all of which these societies have signally proved their power to ameliorate the horrors of war. The earlier of these, while affording great opportunity for the beneficent work of the societies, were also grand fields of instruction and discipline to the committee, enabling them to store up vast funds of practical knowledge which were to be of great service.

The Sanitary Commission of the United States also served as an excellent example in many respects to the relief societies of Europe, and from it they took many valuable lessons. Thus in 1866 Europe was much better prepared than ever before for the care of those who suffered from the barbarisms of war. She was now ready with some degree of ability to oppose the arms of charity to the arms of violence, and make a kind of war on war itself. Still however there was a lack of centralization. The provincial committees worked separately, and consequently lost force. Notwithstanding these drawbacks, large amounts of money were gathered, and munificent supplies of material brought into store. The Austrian Committee alone collected 2,170,000 francs, and a great supply of all things needed in hospital service. The Central Committee was of great use in facilitating correspondence between the different peoples comprising the Austrian Empire, the bureau maintaining correspondence in eleven different languages.

Italy was not backward in the performance of her duty. She used her abundant resources in the most effectual way. Not only were her provincial societies of relief united for common action, but they received external aid from France and Switzerland. Here was exhibited the first beautiful example of neutral powers interfering in the cause of charity in time of war—instead of joining in the work of destruction, lending their aid to repair its damages. The provincial committees banded together under the Central Committee of Milan. Four squads, comprising well-trained nurses and assistants, were organized and furnished with all necessary material to follow the military ambulances or field hospitals, whose wagons were placed at their disposal.

Thus the committee not only reinforced the sanitary personnel of the army, but greatly increased its supplies. It provided entirely the sanitary material for the Tyrolese volunteers, and afforded relief to the navy, and when the war was over it remained among the wounded. In addition to the supplies this committee afforded, it expended in money not less than 199,064 francs.

But after all it was Germany standing between the two armies which distinguished herself. Since the Conference of 1863 she had been acting on the rule of preparation, and now found herself in readiness for all emergencies. The Central Committee of Berlin was flooded with contributions from the provincial committees. In the eight provinces of Prussia 4,000,000 of thalers were collected, and the other states of Germany were not behind. So munificently did the people bestow their aid, that large storehouses were provided in Berlin and in the provinces for its reception, and at the central depot in Berlin two hundred paid persons, besides a large number of volunteers, and nearly three hundred ladies and misses were employed in classifying, parceling, packing up, and dispatching the goods. Special railroad trains carried material to the points of need. In one train were twenty-six cars laden with 1800 to 2000 cwt. of supplies. Never had private charity, however carefully directed, been able to accomplish such prodigies of benevolence. It was now that the beneficence of the Treaty and the excellence of the organization were manifested. But the committee did not confine itself to sending supplies for the wounded to the seat of war. It established and provisioned refreshment stations for the trains, to which those unable to proceed on the trains to the great hospitals without danger to life, were admitted, nursed and cared for with the tenderest solicitude until they were sufficiently recovered to be removed, or death took them. At the station of Pardubitz from six hundred to eight hundred were cared for daily for two months, and lodging provided for three hundred at night. This example suffices to show the extraordinary results of well-organized plans and concerted action. During the war, the relief societies had also to contend with the terrible scourge of cholera. There can be no estimate of the misery assuaged and deaths prevented by the unselfish zeal and devotion of the wearers of the Red Cross.

In the interval between the wars of 1866 and 1867, and that of 1870-71, the time had been improved by the societies existing under the Geneva Treaty, in adding to their resources in every possible manner. Improvements were made in all articles of sanitary service; excellent treatises regarding the hygiene of the camp and hospital were widely circulated; the press had greatly interested itself in the promulgation of information regarding all matters of interest or instruction pertaining to sanitary effort, and almost universally lent its powerful influence to build up the societies. Ten new societies were formed during this time. In Germany the work of the Red Cross was so thoroughly organized, that at the first signal from Berlin, committees arrived as if by magic at all required points, forming a chain which extended over the whole country, and numbered over two thousand persons. This is more remarkable since Germany was a neutral power. Constant communication was kept up between these committees and the central bureau, and the most perfect order and discipline were maintained. Relief was sent from one or another of these stations as was needed. The state afforded free transport, and the voluntary contributions of the people kept up the supplies of sanitary material, so that there was never any lack or danger of failure. With the government transports, whether by land or water, there went always the agents of the Red Cross, protected by their badges and flag, to wait on the invoices, hasten their progress, see to their being kept in good order, and properly delivered at their destination. Depots of supplies were moved from place to place as exigencies demanded. The greatest care was taken to prevent disorder or confusion, and the best military circumspection and regularity prevailed. The great central depot at Berlin comprised seven sections, viz: Camp material; clothing; dressing, for wounds; surgical apparatus; medicines and disinfectants; food and tobacco; and hospital furnishings. Did space allow, it would be desirable to give statistics of the contributions in money and supplies to this service. Suffice it to say, the humanity of peoples is far beyond that of governments. Governments appropriate immense sums to carry on destructive conflicts, but the work of relief societies the world over, and especially during the war of 1870-71, has shown that the philanthropy of the people equals their patriotism. The sums given to assuage the miseries of the Franco-Prussian war were simply fabulous. In 1863, fears were expressed that there would be difficulty in collecting needful funds and supplies to carry out the designs of the treaty. These misgivings proved groundless. After the war of 1870-71, notwithstanding nothing had been withheld in the way of relief, the societies settled their accounts with large balances in their treasuries.

In France not nearly so much had been previously done to provide for the exigencies which fell upon them, but the committee worked with such vigor and so wrought upon the philanthropy of individuals, that active measures of relief were instantly taken. Gold and supplies poured into the hands of the committee at Paris. One month sufficed to organize and provide seventeen campaign ambulances or field hospitals, which immediately joined the army and accompanied it through the first period of the war, or until the battle of Sedan. In Paris ambulances were stationed at the railroad depots to pick up the wounded, and a bureau of information was created for soldiers' families. When the siege of Paris was about to take place, the committee threw, without delay, a commission into Brussels charged with the direction and help of flying hospitals. Nine committees were established in the provinces, with power to act for the Central Committee and to invite the people to help. Meanwhile the committee in Paris did its utmost to mitigate the distress that reigned there, and to prepare for the result of the siege. History has recorded the sufferings, the horrors of misery that accompanied and followed that siege; but history can never relate what wretchedness was averted, what agonies were alleviated, what multitudes of lives were saved, by the presence and effort of the relief societies! What the state of France must have been without the merciful help of the Red Cross societies the imagination dare not picture. After the armistice was signed there were removed from Paris, under the auspices of the relief societies, ten thousand wounded men, who otherwise must have lingered in agony, or died from want of care; and there were brought back by them to French soil nine thousand men who had been cared for in German hospitals.

A Chapter from
The Red Cross in War and Peace, 1898

OUR LADY
OF THE RED CROSS

By Mary R. Parkman

A Christmas baby! Now isn't that the best kind of a Christmas gift for us all?" cried Captain Stephen Barton, who took the interesting flannel bundle from the nurse's arms and held it out proudly to the assembled family.

No longed-for heir to a waiting kingdom could have received a more royal welcome than did that little girl who appeared at the Barton home in Oxford, Massachusetts, on Christmas Day, 1821. Ten years had passed since a child had come to the comfortable farm-house, and the four big brothers and sisters were very sure that they could not have had a more precious gift than this Christmas baby. No one doubted that she deserved a distinguished name, but it was due to Sister Dorothy, who was a young lady of romantic seventeen and something of a reader, that she was called Clarissa Harlowe, after a well-known heroine of fiction. The name which this heroine of real life actually bore and made famous, however, was Clara Barton; for the Christmas baby proved to be a gift not only to a little group of loving friends, but also to a great nation and to humanity.

The sisters and brothers were teachers rather than playmates for Clara, and her education began so early that she had no recollection of the way they led her toddling steps through the beginnings of book-learning. On her first day at school she announced to the amazed teacher who tried to put a primer into her hands that she could spell the "artichoke words." The teacher had other surprises besides the discovery that this mite of three was acquainted with three-syllabled lore.

Brother Stephen, who was a wizard with figures, had made the sums with which he covered her slate seem a fascinating sort of play at a period when most infants are content with counting the fingers of one hand. All other interests, however, paled before the stories that her father told her of great men and their splendid deeds.

Captain Barton was amused one day at the discovery that his precocious daughter, who always eagerly encored his tales of conquerors and leaders, thought of their greatness in images of quite literal and realistic bigness. A president must, for instance, be as large as a house, and a vice-president as spacious as a barn door at the very least. But these somewhat crude conceptions did not put a check on the epic recitals of the retired officer, who, in the intervals of active service in plowed fields or in pastures where his thoroughbreds grazed with their mettlesome colts, liked to live over the days when he served under "Mad Anthony" Wayne in the Revolutionary War, and had a share in the thrilling adventures of the Western frontier.

Clara was only five years old when Brother David taught her to ride. "Learning to ride is just learning a horse," said this daring youth, who was the "Buffalo Bill" of the surrounding country.

"How can I learn a horse, David?" quavered the child, as the high-spirited animals came whinnying to the pasture bars at her brother's call.

"Catch hold of his mane, Clara, and just feel the horse a part of yourself—the big half for the time being," said David, as he put her on the back of a colt that was broken only to bit and halter, and, easily springing on his favorite, held the reins of both in one hand, while he steadied the small sister with the other by seizing hold of one excited foot.

They went over the fields at a gallop that first day, and soon little Clara and her mount understood each other so well that her riding feats became almost as far-famed as those of her brother. The time came when her skill and confidence on horseback—her power to feel the animal she rode a part of herself and keep her place in any sort of saddle through night-long gallops—meant the saving of many lives.

David taught her many other practical things that helped to make her steady and self-reliant in the face of emergencies. She learned, for instance, to drive a nail straight, and to tie a knot that would hold. Eye and hand were trained to work together with quick decision that made for readiness and efficiency in dealing with a situation, whether it meant the packing of a box, or first-aid measures after an accident on the skating-pond.

She was always an outdoor child, with dogs, horses, and ducks for playfellows. The fuzzy ducklings were the best sort of dolls. Sometimes when wild ducks visited the pond and all her waddling favorites began to flap their wings excitedly, it seemed that her young heart felt, too, the call of large, free spaces.

"The only real fun is to do things," she used to say.

She rode after the cows, helped in the milking and churning, and followed her father about, dropping potatoes in their holes or helping weed the garden. Once, when the house was being painted, she begged to be allowed to assist in the work, even learning to grind the pigments and mix the colors. The family was at first amused and then amazed at the persistency of her application as day after day she donned her apron and fell to work.

They were not less astonished when she wanted to learn the work of the weavers in her brothers' satinet mills. At first, her mother refused this extraordinary request; but Stephen, who understood the intensity of her craving to do things, took her part; and at the end of her first week at the flying shuttle Clara had the satisfaction of finding that her cloth was passed as first-quality goods. Her career as a weaver was of short duration, however, owing to a fire which destroyed the mills.

The young girl was as enthusiastic in play as at work. Whether it was a canter over the fields on Billy while her dog, Button, dashed along at her side, his curly white tail bobbing ecstatically, or a coast down the rolling hills in winter, she entered into the sport of the moment with her whole heart.

When there was no outlet for her superabundant energy, she was genuinely unhappy. Then it was that a self-consciousness and morbid sensitiveness became so evident that it was a source of real concern to her friends.

"People say that I must have been born brave," said Clara Barton. "Why, I seem to remember nothing but terrors in my early days. I was a shrinking little bundle of fears—fears of thunder, fears of strange faces, fears of my strange self." It was only when thought and feeling were merged in the zest of some interesting activity that she lost her painful shyness and found herself.

When she was eleven years old she had her first experience as a nurse. A fall which gave David a serious blow on the head, together with the bungling ministrations of doctors, who, when in doubt, had recourse only to the heroic treatment of bleeding and leeches, brought the vigorous young brother to a protracted invalidism. For two years Clara was his constant and devoted attendant. She schooled herself to remain calm, cheerful, and resourceful in the presence of suffering and exacting demands. When others gave way to fatigue or "nerves," her wonderful instinct for action kept her, child though she was, at her post. Her sympathy expressed itself in untiring service.

In the years that followed her brother's recovery Clara became a real problem to herself and her friends. The old blighting sensitiveness made her school-days restless and unhappy in spite of her alert mind and many interests.

At length her mother, at her wit's end because of this baffling, morbid strain in her remarkable daughter, was advised by a man of sane judgment and considerable understanding of child nature, to throw responsibility upon her and give her a school to teach.

It happened, therefore, that when Clara Barton was fifteen she "put down her skirts, put up her hair," and entered upon her successful career as a teacher. She liked the children and believed in them, entering enthusiastically into their concerns, and opening the way to new interests. When asked how she managed the discipline of the troublesome ones, she said, "The children give no trouble; I never have to discipline at all," quite unconscious of the fact that her vital influence gave her a control that made assertion of authority unnecessary.

"When the boys found that I was as strong as they were and could teach them something on the playground, they thought that perhaps we might discover together a few other worth-while things in school hours," she said.

For eighteen years Clara Barton was a teacher. Always learning herself while teaching others, she decided in 1852 to enter Clinton Liberal Institute in New York as a pupil for graduation, for there was then no college whose doors were open to women. When she had all that the Institute could give her, she looked about for new fields for effort.

In Bordentown, New Jersey, she found there was a peculiar need for some one who would bring to her task pioneer zeal as well as the passion for teaching. At that time there were no public schools in the town or, indeed, in the State.

"The people who pose as respectable are too proud and too prejudiced to send their boys and girls to a free pauper school, and in the meantime all the children run wild," Miss Barton was told.

"We have tried again and again," said a discouraged young pedagogue. "It is impossible to do anything in this place."

"Give me three months, and I will teach free," said Clara Barton.

This was just the sort of challenge she loved. There was something to be done. She began with six unpromising gamins in a dilapidated, empty building. In a month her quarters proved too narrow. Each youngster became an enthusiastic and effectual advertisement. As always, her success lay in an understanding of her pupils as individuals, and a quickening interest that brought out the latent possibilities of each. The school of six grew in a year to one of six hundred, and the thoroughly converted citizens built an eight-room school-house where Miss Barton remained as principal and teacher until a breakdown of her voice made a complete rest necessary.

The weak throat soon made it evident that her teaching days were over; but she found at the same time in Washington, where she had gone for recuperation, a new work.

"Living is doing," she said. "Even while we say there is nothing we can do, we stumble over the opportunities for service that we are passing by in our tear-blinded self-pity."

The over-sensitive girl had learned her lesson well. Life offered moment by moment too many chances for action for a single worker to turn aside to bemoan his own particular condition.

The retired teacher became a confidential secretary in the office of the Commissioner of Patents. Great confusion existed in the Patent Office at that time because some clerks had betrayed the secrets of certain inventions. Miss Barton was the first woman to be employed in a Government department; and while ably handling the critical situation that called for all her energy and resourcefulness, she had to cope not only with the scarcely veiled enmity of those fellow-workers who were guilty or jealous, but also with the open antagonism of the rank and file of the clerks, who were indignant because a woman had been placed in a position of responsibility and influence. She endured covert slander and deliberate disrespect, letting her character and the quality of her work speak for themselves. They spoke so eloquently that when a change in political control caused her removal, she was before long recalled to straighten out the tangle that had ensued.

At the outbreak of the Civil War Miss Barton was, therefore, at the very storm-center.

The early days of the conflict found her binding up the wounds of the Massachusetts boys who had been attacked by a mob while passing through Baltimore, and who for a time were quartered in the Capitol. Some of these recruits were boys from Miss Barton's own town who had been her pupils, and all were dear to her because they were offering their lives for the Union. We find her with other volunteer nurses caring for the injured, feeding groups who gathered about her in the Senate Chamber, and, from the desk of the President of the Senate, reading them the home news from the Worcester papers.

Meeting the needs as they presented themselves in that time of general panic and distress, she sent to the Worcester "Spy" appeals for money and supplies. Other papers took up the work, and soon Miss Barton had to secure space in a large warehouse to hold the provisions that poured in.

Not for many days, however, did she remain a steward of supplies. When she met the transports which brought the wounded into the city, her whole nature revolted at the sight of the untold suffering and countless deaths which were resulting from delay in caring for the injured. Her flaming ardor, her rare executive ability, and her tireless persistency won for her the confidence of those in command, and, though it was against all traditions, to say nothing of iron-clad army regulations, she obtained permission to go with her stores of food, bandages, and medicines to the firing-line, where relief might be given on the battle-field at the time of direst need. The girl who had been a "bundle of fears" had grown into the woman who braved every danger and any suffering to carry help to her fellow-countrymen.

People who spoke of her rare initiative and practical judgment had little comprehension of the absolute simplicity and directness of her methods. She managed the sulky, rebellious drivers of her army-wagons, who had little respect for orders that placed a woman in control, in the same way that she had managed children in school. Without relaxing her firmness, she spoke to them courteously, and called them to share the warm dinner she had prepared and spread out in appetizing fashion. When, after clearing away the dishes, she was sitting alone by the fire, the men returned in an awkward, self-conscious group.

"We didn't come to get warm," said their spokesman, as she kindly moved to make room for them at the flames, "we come to tell you we are ashamed. The truth is we didn't want to come. We know there is fighting ahead, and we've seen enough of that for men who don't carry muskets, only whips; and then we've never seen a train under charge of a woman before, and we couldn't understand it. We've been mean and contrary all day, and you've treated us as if we'd been the general and his staff, and given us the best meal we've had in two years. We want to ask your forgiveness, and we sha'n't trouble you again."

She found that a comfortable bed had been arranged for her in her ambulance, a lantern was hanging from the roof, and when next morning she emerged from her shelter, a steaming breakfast awaited her and a devoted corps of assistants stood ready for orders.

"I had cooked my last meal for my drivers," said Clara Barton. "These men remained with me six months through frost and snow and march and camp and battle; they nursed the sick, dressed the wounded, soothed the dying, and buried the dead; and, if possible, they grew kinder and gentler every day."

An incident that occurred at Antietam is typical of her quiet efficiency. According to her directions, the wounded were being fed with bread and crackers moistened in wine, when one of her assistants came to report that the entire supply was exhausted, while many helpless ones lay on the field unfed. Miss Barton's quick eye had noted that the boxes from which the wine was taken had fine Indian meal as packing. Six large kettles were at once unearthed from the farm-house in which they had taken quarters, and soon her men were carrying buckets of hot gruel for miles over the fields where lay hundreds of wounded and dying. Suddenly, in the midst of her labors, Miss Barton came upon the surgeon in charge sitting alone, gazing at a small piece of tallow candle which flickered uncertainly in the middle of the table.

"Tired, Doctor?" she asked sympathetically.

"Tired indeed!" he replied bitterly; "tired of such heartless neglect and carelessness. What am I to do for my thousand wounded men with night here and that inch of candle all the light I have or can get?"

Miss Barton took him by the arm and led him to the door, where he could see near the barn scores of lanterns gleaming like stars.

"What is that!" he asked amazedly.

"The barn is lighted," she replied, "and the house will be directly."

"Where did you get them!" he gasped.

"Brought them with me."

"How many have you?"

"All you want—four boxes."

The surgeon looked at her for a moment as if he were waking from a dream; and then, as if it were the only answer he could make, fell to work. And so it was invariably that she won her complete command of people as she did of situations, by always proving herself equal to the emergency of the moment.

Though, as she said in explaining the tardiness of a letter, "my hands complain a little of unaccustomed hardships," she never complained of any ill, nor allowed any danger or difficulty to interrupt her work.

"What are my puny ailments beside the agony of our poor shattered boys lying helpless on the field?" she said. And so, while doctors and officers wondered at her unlimited capacity for prompt and effective action, the men who had felt her sympathetic touch and effectual aid loved and revered her as "The Angel of the Battlefield."

One incident well illustrates the characteristic confidence with which she moved about amid scenes of terror and panic. At Fredericksburg, when "every street was a firing-line and every house a hospital," she was passing along when she had to step aside to allow a regiment of infantry to sweep by. At that moment General Patrick caught sight of her, and, thinking she was a bewildered resident of the city who had been left behind in the general exodus, leaned from his saddle and said reassuringly:

"You are alone and in great danger, madam. Do you want protection?"

Miss Barton thanked him with a smile, and said, looking about at the ranks, "I believe I am the best-protected woman in the United States."

The soldiers near overheard and cried out, "That's so! that's so!" And the cheer that they gave was echoed by line after line until a mighty shout went up as for a victory.

The courtly old general looked about comprehendingly, and, bowing low, said as he galloped away, "I believe you are right, madam."

Clara Barton was present on sixteen battle-fields; she was eight months at the siege of Charleston, and served for a considerable period in the hospitals of Richmond.

When the war was ended and the survivors of the great armies were marching homeward, her heart was touched by the distress in many homes where sons and fathers and brothers were among those listed as "missing." In all, there were 80,000 men of whom no definite report could be given to their friends. She was assisting President Lincoln in answering the hundreds of heartbroken letters, imploring news, which poured in from all over the land when his tragic death left her alone with the task. Then, as no funds were available to finance a thorough investigation of every sort of record of States, hospitals, prisons, and battle-fields, she maintained out of her own means a bureau to prosecute the search.

Four years were spent in this great labor, during which time Miss Barton made many public addresses, the proceeds of which were devoted to the cause. One evening in the winter of 1868, while in the midst of a lecture, her voice suddenly left her. This was the beginning of a complete nervous collapse. The hardships and prolonged strain had, in spite of her robust constitution and iron will, told at last on the endurance of that loyal worker.

When able to travel, she went to Geneva, Switzerland, in the hope of winning back her health and strength. Soon after her arrival she was visited by the president and members of the "International Committee for the Relief of the Wounded in War," who came to learn why the United States had refused to sign the Treaty of Geneva, providing for the relief of sick and wounded soldiers. Of all the civilized nations, our great republic alone most unaccountably held aloof.

Miss Barton at once set herself to learn all she could about the ideals and methods of the International Red Cross, and during the Franco-Prussian War she had abundant opportunity to see and experience its practical working on the battle-field.

At the outbreak of the war in 1870 she was urged to go as a leader, taking the same part that she had borne in the Civil War.

"I had not strength to trust for that," said Clara Barton, "and declined with thanks, promising to follow in my own time and way; and I did follow within a week. As I journeyed on," she continued, "I saw the work of these Red Cross societies in the field accomplishing in four months under their systematic organization what we failed to accomplish in four years without it—no mistakes, no needless suffering, no waste, no confusion, but order, plenty, cleanliness, and comfort wherever that little flag made its way—a whole continent marshaled under the banner of the Red Cross. As I saw all this and joined and worked in it, you will not wonder that I said to myself 'if I live to return to my country, I will try to make my people understand the Red Cross and that treaty.'"

Months of service in caring for the wounded and the helpless victims of siege and famine were followed by a period of nervous exhaustion from which she but slowly crept back to her former hold on health. At last she was able to return to America to devote herself to bringing her country into line with the Red Cross movement. She found that traditionary prejudice against "entangling alliances with other powers," together with a singular failure to comprehend the vital importance of the matter, militated against the great cause.

"Why should we make provision for the wounded?" it was said. "We shall never have another war; we have learned our lesson."

It came to Miss Barton then that the work of the Red Cross should be extended to disasters, such as fires, floods, earthquakes, and epidemics—"great public calamities which require, like war, prompt and well-organized help."

Years of devoted missionary work with preoccupied officials and a heedless, short-sighted public at length bore fruit. After the Geneva Treaty received the signature of President Arthur on March 1, 1882, it was promptly ratified by the Senate, and the American National Red Cross came into being, with Clara Barton as its first president. Through her influence, too, the International Congress of Berne adopted the "American Amendment," which dealt with the extension of the Red Cross to relief measures in great calamities occurring in times of peace.

The story of her life from this time on is one with the story of the work of the Red Cross during the stress of such disasters as the Mississippi River floods, the Texas famine in 1885, the Charleston earthquake in 1886, the Johnstown flood in 1899, the Russian famine in 1892, and the Spanish-American War. The prompt, efficient methods followed in the relief of the flood sufferers along the Mississippi in 1884 may serve to illustrate the sane, constructive character of her work.

Supply centers were established, and a steamer chartered to ply back and forth carrying help and hope to the distracted human creatures who stood "wringing their hands on a frozen, fireless shore—with every coal-pit filled with water." For three weeks she patrolled the river, distributing food, clothing, and fuel, caring for the sick, and, in order to establish at once normal conditions of life, providing the people with many thousands of dollars' worth of building material, seeds, and farm implements, thus making it possible for them to help themselves and in work find a cure for their benumbing distress.

"Our Lady of the Red Cross" lived past her ninetieth birthday, but her real life is measured by deeds, not days. It was truly a long one, rich in the joy of service. She abundantly proved the truth of the words: "We gain in so far as we give. If we would find our life, we must be willing to lose it."

A Chapter from
Heroines of Service, 1921

SARAH EMMA EDMONDS

1841 — 1898

THE NURSE SPY

Excerpts of Chapters from
Nurse and Spy in the Union Army, 1865

By S. Emma E. Edmonds

EARLY in the spring of 1861, I was returning from the far West, and as I sat waiting for the train which was to bear me to my adopted home in New England, and was meditating upon the events which had transpired during the past few months, the record of which was destined to blacken the fair pages of American history, I was aroused from my reverie by a voice in the street crying "New York Herald—Fall of Fort Sumter—President's Proclamation—Call for seventy-five thousand men!" This announcement startled me, while my imagination portrayed the coming struggle in all its fearful magnitude. War, civil war, with all its horrors seemed inevitable, and even then was ready to burst like a volcano upon the most happy and prosperous nation the sun ever shone upon. The contemplation of this sad picture filled my eyes with tears and my heart with sorrow.

It is true, I was not an American—I was not obliged to remain here during this terrible strife—I could return to my native land where my parents would welcome me to the home of my childhood, and my brothers and sisters would rejoice at my coming. But these were not the thoughts which occupied my mind. It was not my intention, or desire, to seek my own personal ease and comfort while so much sorrow and distress filled the land. But the great question to be decided, was, what can I do? What part am I to act in this great drama? I was not able to decide for myself—so I carried this question to the Throne of Grace, and found a satisfactory answer there.

Five years previous to the time of which I write, I left my rural home, not far from the banks of the St. John's River, in the Province of New Brunswick, and made my way to the United States. An insatiable thirst for education led me to do this, for I believed then, as now, that the "Foreign Missionary" field was the one in which I must labor, sooner or later. I came here a stranger, with but little to recommend me to the favorable notice of the good people, except a letter from the Pastor of the church to which I belonged, and one from my class-leader—notwithstanding, I found kind friends to help me in all my undertakings, and whether in business, education, or spiritual advancement, I have been assisted beyond my highest expectation. I thank God that I am permitted in this hour of my adopted country's need to express a tithe of the gratitude which I feel toward the people of the Northern States.

Ten days after the President's proclamation was issued, I was ready to start for Washington, having been employed by the Government, and furnished with all the necessary equipments. I was not merely to go to Washington and remain there until a battle had been fought and the wounded brought in, and then in some comfortable hospital sit quietly and fan the patients, after the Surgeon had dressed their wounds; but I was to go to the front and participate in all the excitement of the battle scenes, or in other words, be a "Field Nurse."

The great West was stirred to its center, and began to look like a vast military camp. Recruiting offices were filled with men eager to enroll their names as defenders of their country—and women were busily engaged in preparing all the comforts that love and patriotism could suggest, for those who were so soon to go forth to victory or to death, while the clash of arms and strains of martial music almost drowned the hum of industry, and war became the theme of every tongue.

About this time I witnessed the departure of the first western troops which started for Washington. The regiments were drawn up in line—fully equipped for their journey—with their bright bayonets flashing in the morning sunlight. It was on the principal street of a pleasant little village of about a thousand inhabitants, where there was scarcely a family who had not a father, husband, son, or brother in that little band of soldiers who stood there ready to bid them farewell, perhaps for years—perhaps forever. A farewell address was delivered by the village Pastor, and a new Testament presented to each soldier, with the following inscription: "Put your trust in God—and keep your powder dry." Then came the leave-taking—but it is too painful to dwell upon—the last fond word was spoken, the last embrace given, then came the order "march"—and amid the cheers of the citizens—with banners proudly floating, and the bands playing "The Star Spangled Banner," they moved forward on their way to the Capital. On looking back now upon the scenes of that morning, notwithstanding I have looked upon others much more thrilling since then, yet I cannot recall that hour without feelings of deep emotion. While I stood there and beheld those manly forms convulsed with emotion, and heard the sobs of those whom they were leaving behind, I could only thank God that I was free and could go forward and work, and was not obliged to stay at home and weep. A few hours more, and I, too, was on my way to Washington.

When I reached Baltimore I found the city in an uproar—mobs were gathered in the streets and the utmost excitement prevailed: and as the crowded cars moved through the city toward the depot, the infuriated mob threw showers of stones, brickbats, and other missiles, breaking the windows and wounding some of the soldiers. Some of the men could not forbear firing into the crowd—notwithstanding their orders were to the contrary—however, it had a good effect, for the mob soon dispersed; they probably had not forgotten the Sixth Massachusetts and the Pennsylvania troops which had passed through a short time before. The cars soon reached the depot, and started immediately for Washington—where we arrived in due time—weary, and in great need of food and sleep.

Soon after reaching Washington I commenced visiting the temporary hospitals which were prepared to receive the soldiers who arrived there sick. The troops came pouring in so fast, and the weather being extremely warm, all the general hospitals were soon filled, and it seemed impossible to prepare suitable, or comfortable, accommodations for all who required medical attention.

There are many things in connection with this war that we are disposed to find fault with, and we think the blame rests upon such and such individuals—but after investigating the matter, we find that they are all owing to a combination of circumstances entirely beyond the control of those individuals—and it requires time to bring about the desired results. This has been my experience with regard to the hospital department. After walking through the streets for hours on a sultry southern day in search of one of those temporary hospitals, I would find a number of men there delirious with fever—others had been sun-struck and carried there—but no physician to be found in attendance. Then, I would naturally come to the conclusion that the surgeons were all slack concerning their duty—but upon going to the office of the Surgeon in charge of that department, would find that a certain number of surgeons were detailed every morning to visit those hospitals, and were faithfully performing their duty; but that the number of hospitals and patients were increasing so fast that it required all day to make the tour. Consequently the last ones visited were obliged to wait and suffer—without any blame attaching to the surgeons.

Then another great evil was to be remedied—there were thousands of sick men to be taken care of—but for these the Government had made no provision as regards more delicate kinds of food—nothing but hard bread, coffee and pork, for sick and well, alike. The Sanitary Commission had not yet come into operation and the consequence was our poor sick soldiers suffered unspeakably from want of proper nourishment. I was speaking upon this subject one day to Chaplain B. and his wife—my constant companions in hospital labor—when Mrs. B. suggested that she and I should appeal to the sympathies of the ladies of Washington and Georgetown, and try our hand at begging. I agreed to the proposal at once, and wondered why I had not thought of it myself—among all my schemes for alleviating the sufferings of these men, it had never entered into my head to *beg* for them. We decided to go to Georgetown first and if we succeeded there, to canvass Washington. So we started, and commenced operations by calling first upon a clergyman's wife. We made inquiry there with regard to our prospects of success, and the sentiments of the ladies generally upon the war question, and finding that the majority were in our favor, we started again quite hopefully—but not until the lady above mentioned had given us an order on her grocer to the amount of five dollars. I gave Sister B. the credit of that, for I had introduced her as the wife of the Rev. Mr. B., chaplain of the 7th. Then I suggested that we should separate for a few hours—she to take one street and I another, so that we might sooner get through the city. My next call was at a doctor's mansion, but I did not find the lady at home; however, I learned that the doctor in question kept a drug-store near by; she might be there; went, but found no lady; thought fit to make my business known to the doctor, and the consequence was, half a dozen bottles of blackberry wine and two of lemon syrup, with a cordial invitation to call again. So prospered our mission throughout the day, and at the close of it we had a sufficient supply of groceries, brandy, ice, jellies, etc., to fill our little ambulance; and oh, what a change those little delicacies wrought upon our poor sick boys. We were encouraged by that day's work, to continue our efforts in that direction, and finally made Dr. W.'s store a depot for the donations of those kind friends who wished to assist us in restoring to health the defenders of our beloved country.

Typhoid fever began to make its appearance in camp, as the burning sun of June came pouring down upon us, and the hospitals were soon crowded with its victims. It was then that my labors began in earnest, and as I went from tent to tent, ministering to the wants of those delirious, helpless men, I wondered if there ever was a "Missionary Field" which promised a richer harvest, than the one in which I was already engaged; and oh, how thankful I was that it was my privilege to take some small part in so great a work.

I shall notice, briefly, the manner in which the hospitals are conducted in camp. There are large tents furnished for hospital purposes, which will accommodate from twenty to twenty-five men. These tents are usually put up in the most pleasant and shady part of the camp; the inside is nicely leveled, and board floors laid, if boards can be procured, if not, rubber blankets are laid down instead. Sometimes there are straw ticks and cot bedsteads furnished, but not in sufficient quantity to supply all the hospitals. Along each side of the tent the sick are laid, on blankets or cots, leaving room to pass between the beds. In the center of the tent stands a temporary board table, on which are kept books, medicines, et cetera. The hospital corps consists of a surgeon, an assistant surgeon, a hospital steward, a ward-master, four nurses, two cooks, and a man of all work to carry water, cut wood, and make himself generally useful. The immediate care of the sick devolves upon those four nurses, who are generally detailed from the ranks, each one being on duty six hours without intermission. The surgeons visit the patients twice every day, oftener if required; the prescriptions are filled by the hospital steward, and the medicine is administered by the nurses. The nurses are usually very kind to the sick, and when off duty in the hospital, spend much of their time in digging drains around the tents, planting evergreens, and putting up awnings, all of which add much to the coolness and comfort of the hospital. Draining the grounds is a very important part of hospital duty, for when those terrible thunder-storms come, which are so frequent in the south, it is morally impossible to keep the tent floors from being flooded, unless there are drains all around the tents. Great excitement prevails in camp during those tempests—the rain comes down in torrents, while the wind blows a hurricane—lifting the tents from the ground, and throwing everything into wild confusion. I have seen a dozen men stand for hours around one hospital, holding down the ropes and tent poles to prevent the sick from being exposed to the raging elements.

In one of those storms, I saw a tent blown down, in which one of our officers lay suffering from typhoid fever. We did our best to keep him dry until a stretcher could be procured, but all in vain. Notwithstanding we wrapped him in rubber blankets and shawls, yet the rain penetrated them all, and by the time he was carried to a house, a quarter of a mile distant, he was completely drenched. He was a noble fellow and I love to speak of him. Mrs. B. and I remained with him alternately until he died, which was five days from that time. We sent for his wife, who arrived just in time to see him die. He was unconscious when she came, and we were standing around his cot watching every shadow which the sable wing of advancing death cast upon his features, and eagerly looking for a single ray of returning reason. He looked up suddenly, and seeing his wife standing weeping, he beckoned her to come to him. Kneeling beside him, she bent her ear close to the lips of the dying man. He whispered distinctly, "I am going—the way is bright, don't weep—farewell!" A little later he was asked, "What is the foundation of your hope of Heaven?" His face was calm and beautiful in its expression, and his splendid dark eyes lit up with holy confidence and trust, as he replied, "Christ—Christ!" These were his last words. Glorious words for a dying soldier. He lingered a few hours, and then quietly and peacefully breathed out his life. So passed away one of the most exemplary men it has ever been my lot to meet, either in the army or elsewhere. The same day, the sorrowing widow, with the remains of her beloved and noble husband, started for her northern home; and that christian patriot now sleeps in a beautiful little cemetery near the city of Detroit, Michigan, having rendered up his life a willing sacrifice for his country.

Mrs. B. was desirous of visiting some of the public buildings in Washington and wished me to accompany her. I did so, but found that it was almost impossible to get along through the crowded streets. The gallant troops were coming in by thousands from every loyal State in the Union. The Capitol and White House were common places of resort for soldiers. Arms were stacked in the rotunda of the one and the lobbies of the other, while our "noble boys in blue" lounged in the cushioned seats of members of Congress, or reclined in easy chairs in the President's Mansion.

Camps of instruction were prepared near the city, while every hillside and valley for miles around was thickly dotted with snow white tents. Soldiers drilling, fatigue parties building forts, artillery practicing, and the supply trains moving to and from the various headquarters, presented a picture deeply interesting. As I rode from camp to camp and contemplated that immense army concentrating its force on the banks of the Potomac, and saw with what zeal and enthusiasm the soldiers entered upon their duties, I could but feel assured of the speedy termination of the conflict, and look forward with eager anticipation to the day when that mighty host would advance upon the enemy, and like an overwhelming torrent sweep rebellion from the land.

* * * * *

SINCE I returned to New England there have been numerous questions asked me with regard to hospitals, camp life, etc., which have not been fully answered in the preceding narrative, and I have thought that perhaps it would not be out of place to devote a chapter to that particular object.

One great question is: "Do the soldiers get the clothing and delicacies which we send them—or is it true that the surgeons, officers and nurses appropriate them to their own use?"

In reply to this question I dare not assert that all the things which are sent to the soldiers are faithfully distributed, and reach the individuals for whom they were intended. But I have no hesitation in saying that I have reason to believe that the cases are very rare where surgeons or nurses tamper with those articles sent for the comfort of the sick and wounded.

If the ladies of the Soldiers' Aid Societies and other benevolent organizations could have seen even the quantity which I have seen with my own eyes distributed, and the smile of gratitude with which those supplies are welcomed by the sufferers, they would think that they were amply rewarded for all their labor in preparing them.

Just let those benevolent hearted ladies imagine themselves in my place for a single day; removing blood-clotted and stiffened woollen garments from ghastly wounds, and after applying the sponge and water remedy, replacing those coarse, rough shirts by nice, cool, clean linen ones, then dress the wounds with those soft white bandages and lint; take from the express box sheet after sheet, and dainty little pillows with their snowy cases, until you have the entire hospital supplied and every cot looking clean and inviting to the weary, wounded men—then as they are carried and laid upon those comfortable beds, you will often see the tears of gratitude gush forth, and hear the earnest "God bless the benevolent ladies who send us these comforts."

Then, after the washing and clothing process is gone through with, the nice wine or Boston crackers are brought forward, preserved fruits, wines, jellies, etc., and distributed as the different cases may require.

I have spent whole days in this blessed employment without realizing weariness or fatigue, so completely absorbed would I become in my work, and so rejoiced in having those comforts provided for our brave, suffering soldiers.

Time and again, since I have been engaged in writing this little narrative, I have thrown down my pen, closed my eyes, and lived over again those hours which I spent in ministering to the wants of those noble men, and have longed to go back and engage in the same duties once more.

I look back now upon my hospital labors as being the most important and interesting in my life's history. The many touching incidents which come to my mind as I recall those thrilling scenes make me feel as if I should never be satisfied until I had recorded them all, so that they might never be forgotten. One occurs to my mind now which I must not omit:

"In one of the fierce engagements with the rebels near Mechanicsville, a young lieutenant of a Rhode Island battery had his right foot so shattered by a fragment of shell that on reaching Washington, after one of those horrible ambulance rides, and a journey of a week's duration, he was obliged to undergo amputation.

"He telegraphed home, hundreds of miles away, that all was going on well, and with a soldier's fortitude composed his mind and determined to bear his sufferings alone. Unknown to him, however, his mother—one of those dear reserves of the army—hastened up to join the main force. She reached the city at midnight, and hastened to the hospital, but her son being in such a critical condition, the nurses would have kept her from him until morning. One sat by his side fanning him as he slept, her hand on the feeble, fluctuating pulsations which foreboded sad results. But what woman's heart could resist the pleading of a mother at such a moment? In the darkness she was finally allowed to glide in and take the nurse's place at his side. She touched his pulse as the nurse had done. Not a word had been spoken; but the sleeping boy opened his eyes and said: 'That feels like my mother's hand! Who is this beside me? It is my mother; turn up the gas and let me see mother!' The two loving faces met in one long, joyful, sobbing embrace, and the fondness pent up in each heart wept forth its own language.

"The gallant fellow underwent operation after operation, and at last, when death drew near, and he was told by tearful friends that it only remained to make him comfortable, he said he 'had

looked death in the face too many times to be afraid now,' and
died as gallantly as did the men of the Cumberland."

> When a hero goes
> Unto his last repose,
> When earth's trump of fame shall wake him no more;
> When in the heavenly land
> Another soul doth stand,
> Who perished for a Nation ere he reached the shore;
> Whose eyes should sorrow dim?
> Say, who should mourn for him?

> Mourn for the traitor—mourn
> When honor is forsworn;
> When the base wretch sells his land for gold,
> Stands up unblushingly
> And boasts his perfidy,
> Then, then, O patriots! let your grief be told
> But when God's soldier yieldeth up his breath,
> O mourn ye not for him! it is not death!

Another question is frequently asked me—"Are not the private
soldiers cruelly treated by the officers?" I never knew but a very
few instances of it, and then it was invariably by mean, cowardly
officers, who were not fit to be in command of so many mules. I
have always noticed that the bravest and best fighting officers are
the kindest and most forbearing toward their men.

An interesting anecdote is told of the late brave General
Sedgwick, which illustrates this fact:

"One day, while on a march, one of our best soldiers had fallen
exhausted by fatigue and illness, and lay helpless in the road,
when an officer came dashing along in evident haste to join his
staff in advance.

"It was pitiable to see the effort the poor boy made to drag
his unwilling limbs out of the road. He struggled up only to

sink back with a look that asked only the privilege of lying there undisturbed to die.

"In an instant he found his head pillowed on an arm as gentle as his far-away mother's might have been, and a face bent over him expressive of the deepest pity.

"It is characteristic of our brave boys that they say but little. The uncomplaining words of the soldier in this instance were few, but understood.

"The officer raised him in his arms and placed him in his own saddle, supporting the limp and swaying figure by one firm arm, while with the other he curbed the step of his impatient horse to a gentler pace.

"For two miles, without a gesture of impatience, he traveled in this tedious way, until he reached an ambulance train and placed the sick man in one of the ambulances.

"This was our noble Sedgwick—our brave general of the Sixth Corps—pressed with great anxieties and knowing the preciousness of every moment. His men used to say: 'We all know that great things are to be done, and well done, when we see that earnest figure in its rough blouse hurrying past, and never have we been disappointed in him. He works incessantly, is unostentatious, and when he appears among us all eyes follow him with outspoken blessings.'"

I have often been asked: "Have you ever been on a battle-field before the dead and wounded were removed?" "How did it appear?" "Please describe one."

I have been on many a battle-field, and have often tried to describe the horrible scenes which I there witnessed, but have never yet been able to find language to express half the horrors of such sights as I have seen on those terrible fields.

The Rev. Mr. Alvord has furnished us with a vivid description of a battle-field, which I will give for the benefit of those who wish a true and horrifying description of those bloody fields:

"To-day I have witnessed more horrible scenes than ever before since I have been in the army. Hundreds of wounded had lain since the battle, among rebels, intermingled with heaps of slain—hungering, thirsting, and with wounds inflaming and festering. Many had died simply from want of care. Their last battle was fought! Almost every shattered limb required amputation, so putrid had the wounds become.

"I was angry (I think without sin) at your volunteer surgeons. Those of the army were too few, and almost exhausted. But squads of volunteers, as is usual, had come on without instruments, and without sense enough to set themselves at work in any way, and without any idea of dressing small wounds. They wanted to see amputation, and so, while hundreds were crying for help, I found five of these gentlemen sitting at their ease, with legs crossed, waiting for their expected reception by the medical director, who was, of course, up to his elbows in work with saw and amputating knife. I invited them to assist me in my labors among the suffering, but they had 'not come to nurse'—they were 'surgeons.'

"The disgusting details of the field I need not describe. Over miles of shattered forest and torn earth the dead lie, sometimes in *heaps* and *winrows*—I mean literally! friend and foe, black and white, with distorted features, among mangled and dead horses, trampled in mud, and thrown in all conceivable sorts of places. You can distinctly hear, over the whole field, the hum and hissing of decomposition. Of course you can imagine shattered muskets, bayonets, cartridge-boxes, caps, torn clothing, cannon-balls, fragments of shell, broken artillery, etc. I went over it all just before evening, and after a couple of hours turned away in sickening horror from the dreadful sight. I write in the midst of the dead, buried and unburied—in the midst of hospitals full of dying, suffering men, and weary, shattered regiments."

This is a very mild illustration of some battle-fields, and yet it presents an awful picture.

> O God! this land grows rich in loyal blood
> Poured out upon it to its utmost length!

The incense of a people's sacrifice—
The wrested offering of a people's strength.

It is the costliest land beneath the sun!
'Tis purchaseless! and scarce a rood
But hath its title written clear, and signed
In some slain hero's consecrated blood.

And not a flower that gems its mellowing soil
But thriveth well beneath the holy dew
Of tears, that ease a nation's straining heart
When the Lord of Battles smites it through and through.

Now a word about female nurses who go from the North to take care of the soldiers in hospitals. I have said but little upon this point, but could say much, as I have had ample opportunity for observation.

Many of the noble women who have gone from the New England and other loyal States have done, and are still doing, a work which will engrave their names upon the hearts of the soldiers, as the name of Florence Nightingale is engraved upon the hearts of her countrymen.

It is a strange fact that the more highly cultivated and refined the ladies are, they make all the better nurses. They are sure to submit to inconvenience and privations with a much better grace than those of the lower classes.

It is true we have some sentimental young ladies, who go down there and expect to find everything in drawing-room style, with nothing to do but sit and fan handsome young mustached heroes in shoulder-straps, and read poetry, etc.; and on finding the *real* somewhat different from the *ideal*, which their ardent imaginations had created, they become homesick at once, and declare that they "cannot endure such work as washing private soldiers' dirty faces and combing tangled, matted hair; and, what is more, won't do it." So after making considerable fuss, and trailing round in very long silk skirts for several days, until everybody becomes disgusted, they are politely invited by the surgeon in charge to migrate to some more congenial atmosphere.

But the patriotic, whole-souled, educated woman twists up her hair in a "cleared-for-action" sort of style, rolls up the sleeves of her plain cotton dress, and goes to work washing dirty faces, hands and feet, as if she knew just what to do and how to do it. And when she gets through with that part of the programme, she is just as willing to enter upon some new duty, whether it is writing letters for the boys or reading for them, administering medicine or helping to dress wounds. And everything is done so cheerfully that one would think it was really a pleasure instead of a disagreeable task.

But the medical department is unquestionably the greatest institution in the whole army. I will not attempt to answer all the questions I have been asked concerning it, but will say that there are many true stories, and some false ones, circulated with regard to that indispensable fraternity.

I think I may freely say that there is a shadow of truth in that old story of "whiskey" and "incompetency" which we have so often heard applied to individuals in the medical department, who are intrusted with the treatment, and often the lives of our soldiers.

There is a vast difference in surgeons; some are harsh and cruel—whether it is from habit or insensibility I am not prepared to say—but I know the men would face a rebel battery with less forebodings than they do some of our worthy surgeons.

There is a class who seem to act upon the principle of "no smart no cure," if we may be allowed to judge from the manner in which they twitch off bandages and the scientific twists and jerks given to shattered limbs.

Others again are very gentle and tender with the men, and seem to study how to perform the necessary operations with the least possible pain to the patients.

But the young surgeons, fresh from the dissecting room, when operating in conjunction with our old Western practitioners, forcibly reminded me of the anecdote of the young collegian teaching his grandmother to suck an egg: "We make an incision at the apex and an aperture at the base; then making a vacuum with the tongue and palate, we suffer the contained matter to be protruded into the mouth by atmospheric pressure." "La! how strange!" said his grandmother; "in my day we just made a hole in each end, and then sucked it without half that trouble."

I once saw a young surgeon amputate a limb, and I could think of nothing else than of a Kennebec Yankee whom I once saw carve a Thanksgiving turkey; it was his first attempt at carving, and the way in which he disjointed those limbs I shall never forget.

EXCERPTS OF CHAPTERS FROM
Nurse and Spy in the Union Army, 1865

LINDA RICHARDS

1841 — 1930

LINDA RICHARDS
AS I KNEW HER

An Essay by Agnes B. Joynes

In writing this paper, I have quoted from a hospital diary those passages relating to Miss Richards. They do not do her justice, of course, but written spontaneously as they were, and day by day during my training under her, they may give a better idea of her personality and teaching than anything I could write at the present time. They begin during a visit in Worcester, Mass., in the year 1904, where Miss Richards was then establishing a training school in a State Hospital. It was during the last years of her active hospital life. She was working then, as she had been for many years, to advance the standards of her school, educationally and in every other way; she was also striving as she had been from the beginning, for better facilities for training in the schools. Her work was then, as it had been often, rather single handed, I am afraid. What her patient, uphill labor accomplished may be seen in the best training schools of the country to-day. Greater things, due to her influence, will be seen as the years go by. A few facts regarding Miss Richards' early professional life, which were current among the girls of our school, and which I have recorded, are given in more detail in her book of reminiscences which every nurse in the world should read— and then everybody else May 1,1904. I have almost decided to take the nurse's training, which I have always meant to take some time. One school for nurses here is conducted by no less a personage than Miss Linda Richards, that wonderful American woman and nurse. To train to be a nurse under her supervision what an experience it would be! But the school happens to be in a hospital for the insane. I should be scared to death to work there. However, a friend of mine has gone there to train. I met the enthusiastic young woman to-day, and she told me all about it. Miss Richards, it seems, was the first woman in America to receive a nurse's diploma. She trained under all the hardships that Linda a nurse of that time was called upon to endure, and she did it uncomplainingly, her friends say. At the same time, she saw with her keen mind and sympathetic soul, that many improvements might be made in the interest of the future patient and nurse. She crossed the Atlantic for new ideas in her work. I wish I could remember all I was told of her, but at any rate, she was received very kindly in England by Florence Nightingale, then an invalid, but still with all the interest in nursing that had made her famous years before. The fine opinion which Miss Nightingale formed of the young American woman, upon sight, proved to have been well founded. Miss Richards in her hospital life in England and Scotland came up to all expectations, and more. She has spent her life since in establishing training schools for nurses, bringing each as nearly as possible to the measure of her own fine ideals before going on to the next. What a beautiful woman she must be ! I wish she were in some other kind of place. I think I shall go and talk with her about entering the school, just to see her and to hear her voice. May l, 1904. I begin hospital work to-morrow. I went to the state hospital to-day to talk with Miss Richards. She looked me over with kind, keen eyes, and told me she thought she could make room for me at once if I cared to come. She strongly advised me to take the course. I feel a little scarey about it. I meant to ask her if the patients there ever kill people, and I forgot. Miss Richards makes one forget everything but her own wonderful presence. But I am bound to have my training with her, so there ! I am more or less sensible at times (an original idea of mine, none of my friends having ever suggested it) and I feel quite sure that this is one of the times. May 11th. On duty this morning, after Miss Richards had read to me all the rules of the institution, and had given me some kind advice on her own account. She looked at me long and meaningly when she read that we must never curl our hair. Anyone worthy of the profession, she said, will never wish to be anything but her own simple, neat self. I didn't curl my hair. The feeling against hair of that sort seems so strong here, however, that I expect she will send me to a barber any day she happens to decide that the morale of her school depends upon it. I am always finding myself handicapped one way or another. June 15th. Miss Richards went through our ward just before I came off duty. She looked her sweetest and motherliness. She has a kind word for every one, and the patients all love her. She is a strict disciplinarian, a little fear is mingled with the nurses' love, but love she receives, and respect from everyone. She walks with a little limp, a souvenir, I suppose, of the drudgery done for humanity's sake, that always makes me want to pick her up and carry her through the long corridors which thought would amuse her mightily, I imagine, if she could guess it, she being about a foot taller than I, and heavier in proportion. She looked me over to-day from my feet to my head. She looked hard at my head. Her hand lifted mechanically and smoothed her own glossy hair. She sighed and passed on. "Breakers ahead," as seamen say. June 20th. The not wholly unexpected has happened. To-day Miss Richards advised me, in the kindest, sweetest way possible to smooth my hair down a little. I may get it pulled some day by the patients, she says, and the tighter I keep it, the less chance will there be to get a hold. If a patient ever pulls my hair, I will never live to tell the tale. In class, again, to-day. Miss Richards is probation teacher along with her many other duties. We look eagerly forward to the time when we may sit in the cool class-room and be taught by her. She has had such wonderful experiences and she cannot help occasional reminiscences and we are so glad she cannot. She has a funny little habit of rolling two or three pins about on the table in front of her as she talks. When the pins begin to roll, we draw a long breath and begin to listen. Many a delightful anecdote works its way in among our lessons, none the less interesting because it has a point. To-day she taught us to make surgical dressings sponges and pads. While we were folding sponges she told us pretty little stories of her hospital work in Japan. It seems that the first training school for nurses in that country was established by Miss Richards, and with such good effect that she had the happiness of seeing others started there before she left, to which her own Japanese nurses were called to take charge. But Miss Richards did not tell us all that. She speaks only of her work generally. She is so modest. I was sorry when class was dismissed and we had to return to the ward. I shall be so glad when I am placed in a ward where the patients are really sick. I shall then begin to feel that I am going to be a real nurse some day. Miss Richards tells me that I make a great mistake in thinking this, that I am now in a position to get some of the most valuable experience that a nurse may have, that I not only have the opportunity here to observe the differences in different types of tortured nerves, but that I have an unusual opportunity to learn to sooth those nerves, to minister to the spirit as well as to the body, upon which subject she thinks too much stress cannot be laid. She says unless I can do this I will never be a successful nurse. She seems to believe that though the nurse cannot cure without the physician, she can at any rate kill, in spite of all the physicians in the country. It is not impossible, according to her, that death sometimes occurs, due not directly to disease, but to the effect of poisons (I cannot use technical terms) secreted within the body, not to the shock of the serious surgical operation, but to associated discomfort and fears, which the nurse, had she known how, might have allayed. Fortunately, the patient often has a nurse who by a comforting touch of the hand can temporarily relieve pa;n; and who, by a fine tact can allay the fears. Under her care the wearisome, life-spending restlessness and agony will be broken by little naps of sleep, so little perhaps that the patient could not be convinced that he has been asleep at all. This nurse will not try to convince him. She will simply repeat her treatment, and repeat it, and repeat through the day, through the night, until the naps grow longer and that nameless, terrible thing which is worse than pain and which kills when pain could not, takes its leave. And so she seems to believe that the mission of the insane hospital training school is not to the insane alone. It has a wider scope. If we can learn to sooth nerves tortured as these are tortured here, we can hope to do much better work outside. If we can develop tact enough to allay the ever present and terrible fears of these patients, we can surely restore courage to people only physically ill. If the aches and pains here can be comforted, we need not be afraid to attempt any future case. At the same time, she hints that if we have soul enough to make us willing to do all we can for the comfort of these poor people for their sake alone, we will have no time to worry about our future work, and will probably come out just as well in the end. June 22nd. I believe I am becoming attached to this dreadful place. I at least begin to get individuality among the patients. Now the people about me are developing human faces, upon which the sweetest smiles mingle with those expressions of pain and misery common, I suppose, to the insane. There is an individuality in hair black or brown or golden or snowy-white, shining, curling, straight, lustreless-all kinds of hair; in eyes, beautiful, many of them, but with such a pitiful, haunted look. Individual character stands out clearly in this strange maze, with the most lovable, most appealing traits in it. As Miss Richards has said, the right word does go a long way with them. It is such a happy surprise to find that one occasionally has said the right word. I can trot about the ward quite comfortably now. My blistered feet have been under the care of a chiropodist until they are real feet once more. Miss Richards caught me limping and sent me on duty to have them attended to. She is very kind and particular about the nurses' comfort. She would send a nurse with blistered feet off duty as quickly as she would one with curled hair, or hard heels. January 12th. If we only had less scrub-work to do here, and more time to give to the personal needs of our patients. A colossal "If" stares us in the face whichever way we turn. Miss Richards makes it clear to us that she understands the situation, and encourages us to do the best we can, while she tries at the same time to make us believe that the authority which creates and controls conditions here is all righteous and competent and wise, and that we nurses must never, even in mind, criticize a superior. I hope that her nominal superiors are as true to her as she is to them. January 15th. Miss Richards has a way of nosing out trouble, as she goes through the wards. If ten patients talk at once, she seems to get it all, and to know just which story belongs to which. She has the faculty of picking out from the fanciful stories of which our poor people are capable, the tiny grain of truth. If any faintest complaint of a nurse reaches her ears, I should hate to be that nurse if there were any truth in it whatever. If the complaint is not verified by the nurse in charge (it is not always, and that makes the matter more complicated), or if it happens to be a charge nurse herself, she is simply placed in a succession of other wards among different patients and nurses. If the complaints continue, she goes, and the nurses who tried to shield her either go with her, or are the next under observation. She is weeding the school out. No unsuitable nurse escapes her for any length of time. With the supervision and teaching of such a woman, our school should be the finest in the country in time. I hope the "powers that be" will exert their influence to keep her here as long as they can; then see to it that her successor is as much like her as possible-an intelligent, just, kind, forceful woman, an organizer, an educator and they will have no need to worry about the future of the institution. June 1st (Last year of training). All things considered, I am pleased with the way my patients are getting along. I find that just as Miss Richards has taught us, their feelings and actions reflect our own as a mirror reflects the face, only enlarging considerably upon them. If we allow ourselves to become fretted and nervous, it is of no use to try to conceal it from those supersensitive people. They know it before we do, and they, themselves, become nervous and fretful, only much more so. Every motion of our bodies counts as we do our daily work, and excites or calms them as the case may be. Miss Richards constantly reminds us that quietness is very essential, and that, at the best, the usual hospital ward, or even the private room, is not quiet. Even the! rubber-heeled footfall of the nurses about their routine work, in the corridor outside the room, is very trying to a suffering person, and the occasional unguarded voice of the night nurse can make the night torture to any one accustomed to the absolute quiet of sleeping hours at home. And so in order to maintain anything of the all necessary quietness, the nurse must have understanding and sympathy, and then she must use all the self control she may happen to posses. She assures us, and we have found it true, that in proportion to the self-control which we can use, our movements quiet, our voices gentle, in that proportion will our patients be calm and happy. Soon I shall be taking my general hospital course, and I look forward to that with great pleasure, but I am proud beyond measure to have had my first training under Miss Richards. Nowhere else in the world, I imagine, is there a woman like her in the work to-day. We will always remember her as she sat before us in class, and as she walked along the corridors of our wards, her cheering presence, her smile, her bright, sharp glance taking in every little detail as she passed; her whole personality of strength and kindliness. I never knew her to have a favourite. She has severely reprimanded us, one and all, for any delinquency on our part, but at the same time, she has trusted us for meaning well, for being genuine in our interest, as she is herself. She is genuine, along with her other wonderful qualities, and in her genuineness, I imagine, lies her great power.

EDITH CAVELL

1865 — 1915

EDITH LOUISA CAVELL

By Ernest Protheroe

Edith Louisa Cavell was born in 1866 at the country rectory of Swardeston, near Norwich, of which parish her father, the Rev. Frederick Cavell, was rector for forty years. In that pleasant sunny house the little girl passed her early days in uneventful happiness, for Swardeston had few interests apart from the obscurities of its own rural retirement.

The rector, who was a kindly man at heart, but firm to the point of sternness where his duty was concerned, ruled his home with evangelical strictness. His daughter Edith was a thoughtful child; and her unfailing consideration for others and her concern for their welfare caused her to be beloved by everybody. But the child's innate gentleness was tinged with a sense of duty remarkable in one of her years, which characteristic was the undoubted outcome of her father's precept and example.

Edith Cavell's education was as thorough as her parents could contrive; and, apart from mere scholarship, her outlook was widened by being sent to a school at Brussels.

When the Rev. Frederick Cavell died, the family removed from Swardeston to Norwich, and Edith decided to adopt the profession of nursing the sick poor. To that end on September 3, 1895, she entered the London Hospital as a probationer, and remained in that great institution for nearly five years.

From the first, by her unselfish devotion to duty she endeared herself to her colleagues and patients alike. Part of the time she was staff nurse in the 'Mellish' Ward; and when the authorities sent her to Maidstone at the great outbreak of typhoid in that

151

town, she did excellent work.

Later, Miss Cavell was appointed to the post of night superintendent at St. Pancras Infirmary, where she remained for three years; then she migrated to Shoreditch Infirmary to act as assistant superintendent. As evidence of her more than ordinarily wide experience, it should be stated that for a time she worked at Fountain Hospital, Lower Tooting, under the Metropolitan Asylums Board; and for nine months she acted temporarily as matron of the Ashton New Road District Home, Manchester.

In all these varied spheres of activity Nurse Cavell proved herself not only a capable nurse, but she became a clever, painstaking teacher, able to illustrate her eloquent lectures by means of her own facile and useful diagrams. Many nurses acknowledge their indebtedness to her lucid teaching, and are proud to claim their one-time association with one whose devotion and energy made her an ornament of a noble profession.

The sense of duty, which in the child was indicated so plainly, in after years developed into almost a religion. Every one with whom Miss Cavell came in contact speedily understood that she placed duty before either friendship or personal comfort. Her hospital training had taught her the value of discipline, and she would never tolerate inefficiency, or any tendency towards slackness, in her subordinates. As a surgical nurse her skill was remarkable; but her undoubted *forte* was the power of organization, which is almost rare compared to mere cleverness in the technical details of nursing.

Her absorption in her calling and her outwardly stern and reserved demeanour sometimes caused Nurse Cavell to be misunderstood; but those who were fortunate enough to serve under her quickly came to learn to admire her, equally as a nurse and a kind woman. Her expressive eyes were an index to her overflowing sympathy; and her fellow nurses found themselves impelled to take their troubles and difficulties to her, sure of a patient hearing and tactful and sympathetic advice.

In 1906 Miss Cavell was offered and accepted the position

of matron of a surgical and medical home in Brussels, which had been founded by Monsieur de Page. This enlightened and enthusiastic Belgian doctor was impressed by the need of a better knowledge of hygiene and aseptic methods, of which through no fault of their own the nursing sisters in Belgium were generally ignorant.

Nurse Cavell's new post was one that called for the utmost discretion, for she was an Englishwoman and a Protestant, engaging in work which hitherto was practically a monopoly of the Roman Catholic religious sisterhood. But even inborn prejudice, and in some cases positive enmity, could not long hold out against Miss Cavell's professional skill, backed up by her charm of manner; and in quite a short time she was as popular with the Belgian staff and patients as had always proved to be the case in her English experience.

The establishment of a training school for nurses was a bold experiment, for Belgian women of good birth and education were accustomed to look upon earning their own living as a loss of caste.

The English nurse was fully aware of the difficulties with which she had to contend, and resolutely set herself to combat them. Soon she had five pupils, who commenced their work on recognized lines. Their uniform consisted of blue cotton dresses, high white aprons with white linen sleeves to cover the forearm, which was bare beneath, 'Sister Dora' caps without strings, and white collars. 'The contrast,' wrote Miss Cavell to the *Nursing Mirror*, 'the probationers present to the nuns in their heavy stuff robes, and the lay nurses in their grimy apparel, is the contrast of the unhygienic past with the enlightened present. These Belgian probationers in three years' time will look back on the first days of trial with wonder.'

By April, 1908, the probationers had increased to thirteen; and by 1912 the number was thirty-two. Some of the members of the staff were English nurses who had worked in the London Hospital or the Shoreditch Infirmary. They not only assisted in training the probationers, but also attended the private patients in the Nursing Home which was attached to the school.

Miss Cavell's school met with the warm approval of the Queen of the Belgians, who was quick to realize the value of trained nursing in Brussels. When Queen Elizabeth broke her arm a few years ago she did not hesitate to have it attended to by the nurses at the Home. Her Majesty's action was an exceedingly valuable tribute to the institution and the Englishwoman at its head. It gave public opinion a lead that caused the School and Home to be viewed favourably, where, perhaps, hitherto the new departure had been deprecated, if only because it was considered to be an unnecessary rival of the nuns and lay nurses, who worked under religious vows.

The Queen came to hold a very sincere regard for Miss Cavell, and it is certain that the feeling was reciprocated. Little did the royal patient and the English nurse then imagine that within but a few short years they would figure together in adversity, in their respective spheres, as two of the most empathetic heroines in modern history.

Quiet and unassuming, yet determined and courageous, Nurse Cavell continued her good work, which was bound to have a marked effect on the future of the Belgian nursing profession. She herself declared that 'the spread of light and knowledge is bound to follow in years to come. The nurses will not only teach, as none others have the opportunity of doing, the laws of health and the prevention and healing of disease; they will show their countrywomen that education and position do not constitute a bar to an independent life; they are rather a good and solid foundation on which to build a career which demands the best and highest qualities that womanhood can offer.'

In acting as directress of three hospitals, Miss Cavell found full scope even for her unusual organizing capabilities. In addition to her arduous lectures throughout the day, she gave four lectures to the doctors and two to the nurses every week. She always attended at the operating-theatre herself. One of her greatest pleasures was the children's ward, decorated in blue and white after her own design; she made a special point of visiting the little inmates every evening. The better class of Belgians paid for the services of the private staff of nurses, but the call of the poor never went unheeded.

Although Miss Cavell was intensely happy in her work in Brussels, she always looked forward with positive joy to visiting her aged mother, with whom she spent every possible holiday in England. In the summer of 1914 mother and daughter were enjoying one of these affectionate reunions.

Suddenly the great war-cloud burst. Edith Cavell was in her mother's garden weeding a bed of heartsease when she heard the news. She needed no heart-searching to decide where her duty lay; and, without hesitation, she returned hotfoot to Belgium, where she had an intuition that she would be wanted.

A CHAPTER FROM
The Life-Story of Edith Cavell, 1916

THE STORY OF
EDITH CAVELL

By Richard Wilson

There is a lofty, snow-clad peak in the Canadian Rockies which is known by the name of Mount Edith Cavell. It was named in the year 1915 to enshrine the memory of a noble woman who laid down her life for the love of humanity. She was an English patriot, but, as we shall see as we go on with her story, she was much more than that.

Edith Cavell was a hospital nurse who was trained in London and went to Belgium in 1900 to take charge of a training school for nurses in a suburb of Brussels. She threw herself into her work with great devotion and in a few years made it a real success. Then the war began and the Germans marched into Brussels as victors; but Miss Cavell was allowed to stay at her hospital.

The Germans seemed to know that she might be useful even to their own men; and they were not mistaken. The course of events brought many German wounded to Brussels and these men received the same care as the Belgian wounded. All hurt or sick men were the same to Edith Cavell, and her one aim was to get them well again.

After the retreat from Mons and from Namur, a number of French and English soldiers were cut off from the main army and were left behind in Belgium. These men hid themselves in the woods or in the ruins of shattered towns, watching for an opportunity to escape either into France or Holland. Some of them were captured by the Germans, and many were shot at once without any form of trial. Others were taken care of by the country people and many stories could be told, and probably will be told in the future, of the adventures of these refugees in their own land.

There were many Belgians, too, who had been left behind after the earlier battles of the war, and these poor fugitives in their native land had the same experiences. Some were taken and instantly shot; others were dressed in civilian clothing and given work on the land, and when the chance came were helped across the frontier into Holland. Many were shot by the German guards as they made their last dash for freedom across the barbed-wire fence which marked off Holland from Belgium.

There was constant movement among the English, French, and Belgians to get away. Many of them had been brought into touch with Miss Cavell at one or other of her hospitals and they seem to have begged for her help. She had means of helping them and she did not hesitate to use them. She did not count the cost to herself. Here were men who, if taken, would most probably be shot out of hand. What could a good woman do but help them to escape? She would thereby break the German military law, but she would be faithful to the higher law of kindness.

It was afterwards told against her by the Germans that she helped 130 men to leave Belgium. We do not know whether this number is correct, but if it were halved the record would still be a proud one.

After a time the Germans began to be suspicious of Miss Cavell. Spies were ordered to watch her. One of these men, it is said, went to ask her to help him to leave the country; she listened to his story, promised to help him, and then in accordance with his "duty" he betrayed her to his higher officers. She was made a prisoner on the 5th of August 1915.

In the military prison she was closely confined and no one was allowed to see her. She was considered a most dangerous person, as indeed she was when it was a question of mercy and pity before obedience to a brutal law. The Germans tell that she made no effort to hide or excuse the fact that she had helped men to escape from the country. She had acted as she did, knowing full well that she was breaking the rule of the Germans. It was said that she fully expected to be caught some day and to suffer punishment, but that she thought it would take the form of imprisonment for a time.

There was living in Brussels at this time a Mr. Brand Whitlock who was American Minister, that is to say, he was in charge of American affairs in Belgium. As soon as he heard that Miss Cavell had been arrested, he wrote to the German officers and did all he could to get a fair trial for the lady. The Germans said that no one would be allowed to see Miss Cavell, but that she should have a trial in accordance with the soldier's law.

Mr. Whitlock was told that Miss Cavell had said that she was "guilty"; that she had hidden in her house French, English, and Belgians who were anxious to get away from Belgium; and that she had given them money and other help, sometimes providing guides to conduct them to the frontier.

Her trial began on the 7th October, and thirty-four other prisoners were tried with her. The language used in the court was German, and when a question was put to Miss Cavell it was translated into French, with which she was familiar. She was allowed to have a lawyer to speak in her defence, but she did not see him until the day of the trial, so that his help was of no great service to her. She had, however, confessed her "fault," so that it did not matter. She probably thought of cases in English military history where women had been found guilty of military offences and had been imprisoned; and the punishment seemed light when she thought of the young lives that she had saved and of the mothers and sisters and sweethearts who would bless her name until their dying day.

Perhaps she was as much surprised as were many other people when she was sentenced to die. Before sentence was passed upon her she was asked why she had helped soldiers to go to England. She replied quite simply that she thought if she had not done so they would have been shot by the Germans; and she considered she only did her duty to her country in saving their lives. The order of the court was that she should be shot the next morning at two o'clock.

During the following evening the American Minister made almost frantic efforts to save her life. He was nobly helped by the Spanish Minister, but all their efforts were of no avail. Mr. Gahan, the British chaplain in Brussels, was, however, allowed to see Miss Cavell in her prison.

"I found her," he afterwards wrote, "perfectly calm and resigned. She said that she wished her friends to know that she willingly gave her life for her country and said, 'I have no fear nor shrinking; I have seen death so often that it is not strange or fearful to me.'

"She further said, 'I thank God for this ten weeks' quiet before the end. Life has always been hurried and full of difficulty. This time of rest has been a great mercy. They have all been very kind to me here. But this I would say, standing as I do in view of God and eternity, I realise that patriotism is not enough. I must have no hatred or bitterness towards any one.'

"We sat quietly talking until it was time for me to go. She gave me parting messages for relations and friends. Then I said, 'Good-bye,' and she smiled and said, 'We shall meet again.'"

Next morning she was shot. The place of her burial was kept secret, for the Germans feared that the Belgians would make it a rallying place for rebellion. In this way they showed that they knew they had acted not only inhumanly but foolishly.

The execution of Edith Cavell roused great anger throughout the world, except of course in Germany. British and French soldiers fought with greater courage with her name upon their lips. From every civilised country came protests against the shooting of a woman whose only military offence was that she had followed the promptings of a tender heart.

Her story was told in every British school and the Education Minister of France gave orders that the teachers of Paris should also tell it to their pupils. "The great and sublime figure of Edith

Cavell," he said, "stands forth among the black horrors of the war as a living image of outraged humanity." Her death and the way it was regarded in Germany reminded the Allies once again that in fighting Germany they were fighting barbarism and the spirit which aims at "success" at any price.

In our just anger at the executioners of this noble lady let us not miss the true lesson of her splendid life and her heroic death.

She loved England first as became an Englishwoman. That was made quite clear in all that she said and did. She loved the friends of England too—all those who were fighting for the same great cause. That also was perfectly clear.

But mark once more that noble utterance spoken on the last evening of her life, "This I would say, standing as I do in view of God and eternity, *I realise that patriotism is not enough. I must have no hatred or bitterness towards any one.*"

We know that she had helped German wounded and had shown them all the care and tenderness that the sight of a suffering man could arouse in her. She did this, not because she had any desire to help the rulers of Germany whose ways she hated, but because the men were human beings.

Her kindness to German wounded and her last words which are twice quoted above were her woman's protest against the folly and the wickedness of all war. She could put aside with a quiet smile the pompous military rule which laid down that certain things were to be done because men were living in a state of war. She followed a higher rule, the law of pity and of mercy, remembering the words of the great poet of her beloved country:

"Earthly power doth then show likest God's
When mercy seasons justice."

A Chapter from
The Post of Honour –
Stories of Daring Deeds Done by Men of
the British Empire in the Great War, 1917

VIOLETTA THURSTAN

1879 — 1978

THE BEGINNING OF IT ALL
AND OUR WORK IN WARSAW

Excerpts of Chapters from
Field Hospital and Flying Column

By Violetta Thurstan

War, war, war. For me the beginning of the war was a torchlight tattoo on Salisbury Plain. It was held on one of those breathless evenings in July when the peace of Europe was trembling in the balance, and when most of us had a heartache in case—*in case* England, at this time of internal crisis, did not rise to the supreme sacrifice.

It was just the night for a tattoo—dark and warm and still. Away across the plain a sea of mist was rolling, cutting us off from the outside world, and only a few pale stars lighted our stage from above.

The field was hung round with Chinese lanterns throwing weird lights and shadows over the mysterious forms of men and beasts that moved therein. It was fascinating to watch the stately entrance into the field, Lancers, Irish Rifles, Welsh Fusiliers, Grenadiers and many another gallant regiment, each marching into the field in turn to the swing of their own particular regimental tune until they were all drawn up in order.

There followed a very fine exhibition of riding and the usual torchlight tricks, and then the supreme moment came. The massed bands had thundered out the first verse of the Evening Hymn, the refrain was taken up by a single silver trumpet far away—a sweet thin almost unearthly note more to be felt than heard—and then the bands gathered up the whole melody and everybody sang the last verse together.

The Last Post followed, and then I think somehow we all knew.

* * * * *

A week later I had a telegram from the Red Cross summoning me to London.

London was a hive of ceaseless activity. Territorials were returning from their unfinished training, every South Coast train was crowded with Naval Reserve men who had been called up, every one was buying kits, getting medical comforts, and living at the Army and Navy Stores. Nurses trained and untrained were besieging the War Office demanding to be sent to the front, Voluntary Aid Detachment members were feverishly practising their bandaging, working parties and ambulance classes were being organized, crowds without beginning and without end were surging up and down the pavements between Westminster and Charing Cross, wearing little flags, buying every half-hour edition of the papers and watching the stream of recruits at St. Martin's. All was excitement—no one knew what was going to happen. Then the bad news began to come through from Belgium, and every one steadied down and settled themselves to their task of waiting or working, whichever it might happen to be.

I was helping at the Red Cross Centre in Vincent Square, and all day long there came an endless procession of women wanting to help, some trained nurses, many—far too many—half-trained women; and a great many raw recruits, some anxious for adventure and clamouring "to go to the front at once," others willing and anxious to do the humblest service that would be of use in this time of crisis.

Surely after this lesson the Bill for the State Registration of Trained Nurses cannot be ignored or held up much longer. Even now in this twentieth century, girls of twenty-one, nurses so-called with six months' hospital training, somehow manage to get out to the front, blithely undertaking to do work that taxes to its very utmost the skill, endurance, and resource of the most highly trained women who have given up the best years of their life to learning the principles that underlie this most exacting of professions. For it is not only medical and surgical nursing that is learnt in a hospital ward, it is discipline, endurance, making the best of adverse circumstances, and above all the knowledge of mankind. These are the qualities that are needed at the front, and they cannot be imparted in a few bandaging classes or instructions in First Aid.

This is not a diatribe against members of Voluntary Aid Detachments. They do not, as a rule, pretend to be what they are not, and I have found them splendid workers in their own department. They are not half-trained nurses but fully trained ambulance workers, ready to do probationer's work under the fully trained sisters, or if necessary to be wardmaid, laundress, charwoman, or cook, as the case may be. The difficulty does not lie with them, but with the women who have a few weeks' or months' training, who blossom out into full uniform and call themselves Sister Rose, or Sister Mabel, and are taken at their own valuation by a large section of the public, and manage through influence or bluff to get posts that should only be held by trained nurses, and generally end by bringing shame and disrepute upon the profession.

The work in the office was diversified by a trip to Faversham with some very keen and capable Voluntary Aid Detachment members, to help improvise a temporary hospital for some Territorials who had gone sick. And then my turn came for more active service. I was invited by the St. John Ambulance to take out a party of nurses to Belgium for service under the Belgian Red Cross Society.

Very little notice was possible, everything was arranged on Saturday afternoon of all impossible afternoons to arrange anything in London, and we were to start for Brussels at eight o'clock on Tuesday morning.

On Monday afternoon I was interviewing my nurses, saying good-bye to friends—shopping in between—wildly trying to get everything I wanted at the eleventh hour, when suddenly a message came to say that the start would not be to-morrow after all. Great excitement—telephones—wires—interviews. It seemed that there was some hitch in the arrangements at Brussels, but at last it was decided by the St. John's Committee that I should go over alone the next day to see the Belgian Red Cross authorities before the rest of the party were sent off. The nurses were to follow the day after if it could be arranged, as having been all collected in London, it was very inconvenient for them to be kept waiting long.

Early Tuesday morning saw me at Charing Cross Station. There were not many people crossing—two well-known surgeons on their way to Belgium, Major Richardson with his war-dogs, and a few others. A nurse going to Antwerp, with myself, formed the only female contingent on board. It was asserted that a submarine preceded us all the way to Ostend, but as I never get further than my berth on these occasions, I cannot vouch for the truth of this.

Ostend in the middle of August generally means a gay crowd of bathers, Cook's tourists tripping to Switzerland and so on; but our little party landed in silence, and anxious faces and ominous whispers met us on our arrival on Belgian soil. It was even said that the Germans were marching on Brussels, but this was contradicted afterwards as a sensational canard. The Red Cross on my luggage got me through the *douane* formalities without any trouble. I entered the almost empty train and we went to Brussels without stopping.

At first sight Brussels seemed to be *en fête*, flags were waving from every window, Boy Scouts were everywhere looking very important, and the whole population seemed to be in the streets. Nearly every one wore little coloured flags or ribbons—a favourite badge was the Belgian colours with the English and French intertwined. It did not seem possible that war could be so near, and yet if one looked closer one saw that many of the flags giving such a gay appearance were Red Cross flags denoting that there an ambulance had been prepared for the wounded, and the Garde Civile in their picturesque uniform were constantly breaking up the huge crowds into smaller groups to avoid a demonstration.

The first thing to arrange was about the coming of my nurses, whether they were really needed and if so where they were to go. I heard from the authorities that it was highly probable that Brussels *would* be occupied by the Germans, and that it would be best to put off their coming, for a time at any rate. Private telegrams had long been stopped, but an official thought he might be able to get mine through, so I sent a long one asking that the nurses might not be sent till further notice. As a matter of fact it never arrived, and the next afternoon I heard that twenty-six nurses—instead of sixteen as was originally arranged—were already on their way. There were 15,000 beds in Brussels prepared for the reception of the wounded, and though there were not many wounded in the city just then, the nurses would certainly all be wanted soon if any of the rumours were true that we heard on all sides, of heavy fighting in the neighbourhood, and severe losses inflicted on the gallant little Belgian Army.

It was impossible to arrange for the nurses to go straight to their work on arrival, so it was decided that they should go to a hotel for one night and be drafted to their various posts the next day. Anyhow, they could not arrive till the evening, so in the afternoon I went out to the barriers to see what resistance had been made against the possible German occupation of Brussels. It did not look very formidable—some barbed-wire entanglements, a great many stones lying about, and the Gardes Civiles in their quaint old-fashioned costume guarding various points. That was all.

In due time my large family arrived and were installed at the hotel. Then we heard, officially, that the Germans were quite near the city, and that probably the train the nurses had come by would be the last to get through, and this proved to be the case. *Affiches* were pasted everywhere on the walls with the Burgomaster's message to his people:

A Sad Hour!
The Germans are at our Gates!

PROCLAMATION OF THE
BURGOMASTER OF BRUSSELS

Citizens,—In spite of the heroic resistance of our troops, seconded by the Allied Armies, it is to be feared that the enemy may invade Brussels. If this eventuality should take place, I hope that I may be able to count on the calmness and steadiness of the population. Let every one keep himself free from terror—free from panic. The Communal Authorities will not desert their posts. They will continue to exercise their functions with that firmness of purpose that you have the right to demand from them under such grave circumstances. I need hardly remind my fellow-citizens of their duty to their country. The laws of war forbid the enemy to force the population to give information as to the National Army and its method of defence. The inhabitants of Brussels must know that they are within their rights in refusing to give any information on this point to the invader. This refusal is their duty in the interests of their country. Let none of you act as a guide to the enemy. Let every one take precautions against spies and foreign agents, who will try to gather information or provoke manifestations. The enemy cannot legitimately harm the family honour nor the life of the citizens, nor their private property, nor their philosophic or religious convictions, nor interfere with their religious services. Any abuse committed by the invader must be immediately reported to me. As long as I have life and liberty, I shall protect with all my might the dignity and rights of my fellow-citizens. I beg the inhabitants to facilitate my task by abstaining from all acts of hostility, all employment of arms, and by refraining from intervention in battles or encounters. Citizens, whatever happens, listen to the voice of your Burgomaster and maintain your confidence in him; he will not betray it.

Long live Belgium free and independent!
Long live Brussels!

ADOLPHE MAX.

All that night refugees from Louvain and Termonde poured in a steady stream into Brussels, seeking safety. I have never seen a more pitiful sight. Little groups of terror-stricken peasants fleeing from their homes, some on foot, some more fortunate ones with their bits of furniture in a rough cart drawn by a skeleton horse or a large dog. All had babies, aged parents, or invalids with them. I realized then for the first time what war meant. We do not know in England. God grant we never may. It was not merely rival armies fighting battles, it was civilians—men, women, and children—losing their homes, their possessions, their country, even their lives. This invasion of unfortunates seemed to wake Brussels up to the fact that the German army was indeed at her gate. Hordes of people rushed to the Gare du Nord in the early dawn to find it entirely closed, no trains either entering or leaving it. It was said that as much rolling-stock as was possible had been sent to France to prevent it being taken by the Germans. There was then a stampede to the Gare du Midi, from whence a few trains were still leaving the city crammed to their utmost capacity.

In the middle of the morning I got a telephone message from the Belgian Red Cross that the Germans were at the barriers, and would probably occupy Brussels in half an hour, and that all my nurses must be in their respective posts before that time.

Oh dear, what a stampede it was. I told the nurses they must leave their luggage for the present and be ready in five minutes, and in less than that time we left the hotel, looking more like a set of rag-and-bone men than respectable British nursing sisters. One had seized a large portmanteau, another a bundle of clean aprons, another soap and toilet articles; yet another provident soul had a tea-basket. I am glad that the funny side of it did not strike me then, but in the middle of the next night I had helpless hysterics at the thought of the spectacle we must have presented. Mercifully no one took much notice of us—the streets were crowded and we had difficulty in getting on in some places—just at one corner there was a little cheer and a cry of "Vive les Anglais!"

It took a long time before my flock was entirely disposed of. It had been arranged that several of them should work at one of the large hospitals in Brussels where 150 beds had been set apart for the wounded, five in another hospital at the end of the city, two in an ambulance station in the centre of Brussels, nine were taken over to a large fire-station that was converted into a temporary hospital with 130 beds, and two had been promised for a private hospital outside the barriers. It was a work of time to get the last two to their destinations; the Germans had begun to come in by that time, and we had to wait two hours to cross a certain street that led to the hospital, as all traffic had been stopped while the enemy entered Brussels.

It was an imposing sight to watch the German troops ride in. The citizens of Brussels behaved magnificently, but what a bitter humiliation for them to undergo. How should we have borne it, I wonder, if it had been London? The streets were crowded, but there was hardly a sound to be heard, and the Germans took possession of Brussels in silence. First the Uhlans rode in, then other cavalry, then the artillery and infantry. The latter were dog-weary, dusty and travel-stained—they had evidently done some forced marching. When the order was given to halt for a few minutes, many of them lay down in the street just as they were, resting against their packs, some too exhausted to eat, others eating sausages out of little paper bags (which, curiously enough, bore the name of a Dutch shop printed on the outside) washed down with draughts of beer which many of the inhabitants of Brussels, out of pity for their weary state, brought them from the little drinking-houses that line the Chaussée du Nord.

The rear was brought up by Red Cross wagons and forage carts, commissariat wagons, and all the miscellaneous kit of an army on the march. It took thirty-six hours altogether for the army to march in and take possession. They installed themselves in the Palais de Justice and the Hôtel de Ville, having requisitioned beds, food and everything that they wanted from the various hotels. Poor Madame of the Hotel X. wept and wrung her hands over the loss of her beautiful beds. Alas, poor Madame! The next day her husband was shot as a spy, and she cared no longer about the beds.

In the meantime, just as it got dark, I installed my last two nurses in the little ambulance out beyond the barriers.

OUR WORK IN WARSAW

In two or three days' time after our visit to the Empress we were off to Warsaw and reported ourselves to Monsieur Goochkoff, the head of the Red Cross Society there.

We received our marching orders at once. We were not to be together at first, as they thought we should learn Russian more quickly if we were separated, so two of us were to go to one hospital in Warsaw, two to another. My fate was a large Red Cross hospital close to the station, worked by a Community of Russian Sisters. I must say I had some anxious moments as I drove with Sister G. to the hospital that afternoon. I wondered if Monsieur Goochkoff had said we were coming, and thought if two Russian Sisters suddenly turned up without notice at an English hospital how very much surprised they would be. Then I hoped they were very busy, as perhaps then they would welcome our help. But again, I meditated, if they were really busy, we with our stumbling Russian phrases might be only in the way. It was all very well in Denmark to think one would come and help Russia—but supposing they did not want us after all?

By the time I got so far we had arrived at the hospital, the old familiar hospital smell of disinfectants met my nostrils, and I felt at home at once. I found that I had been tormenting myself in vain, for they were expecting us and apparently were not at all displeased at our arrival. The Sister Superior had worked with English people in the Russo-Japanese War and spoke English almost perfectly, and several of the other Sisters spoke French or German. She was very worried as to where we should sleep, as they were dreadfully overcrowded themselves; even she had shared her small room with another Sister. However, she finally found us a corner in a room which already held six Sisters. Eight of us in a small room with only one window! The Sisters sleeping there took our advent like angels, said there was plenty of room, and moved their beds closer together so that we might have more space. Again I wondered whether if it were England we should be quite so amiable under like circumstances. I hope so.

I began to unpack, but there was nowhere to put anything; there was no furniture in the room whatsoever except our straw beds, a table, and a large tin basin behind a curtain in which we all washed—and, of course, the ikon or holy picture which hangs in every Russian room. We all kept our belongings under our beds—not a very hygienic proceeding, but à la guerre comme à la guerre. The patients were very overcrowded too, every corridor was lined with beds, and the sanitars, or orderlies, slept on straw mattresses in the hall. The hospital had been a large college and was originally arranged to hold five hundred patients, but after the last big battle at Soldau every hospital in Warsaw was crammed with wounded, and more than nine hundred patients had been sent in here and had to be squeezed into every available corner.

My work was in the dressing-room, which meant dressing wounds all day and sometimes well into the night, and whatever time we finished there were all the dressings for the next day to be cut and prepared before we could go to bed. The first week was one long nightmare with the awful struggle for the Russian names of dressings and instruments and with their different methods of working, but after that I settled down very happily.

Sister G. was in the operating-room on the next floor, and she, too, found that first week a great strain. The other two Sisters who had come out with us and had been sent to another hospital apparently found the same, for they returned to England after the first five days, much to my disappointment, as I had hoped that our little unit of four might have got a small job of our own later, when we could speak Russian better and had learnt their ways and customs.

After the first few days we began to be very busy. In England we should consider that hospital very badly staffed, as there were only twenty Sisters to sometimes nearly a thousand patients, all very serious cases moreover, as we were not supposed to take in the lightly wounded at all in this hospital. The sanitars, or orderlies, do all that probationers in an English hospital would do for the patients, and all the heavy lifting and carrying, so that the work is not very hard though very continuous. There was no night staff. We all took it in turns to stay up at night three at a time, so that our turn came about once a week. That meant being on duty all day, all night, and all the next day, except for a brief rest and a walk in the afternoon. Most of the Sisters took no exercise beyond one weekly walk, but we two English people longed for fresh air, and went out whenever possible even if it was only for ten minutes. English views on ventilation are not at all accepted in Russia. It is a great concession to open the windows of the ward for ten minutes twice a day to air it, and the Sisters were genuinely frightened for the safety of the patients when I opened the windows of a hot, stuffy ward one night. "It is never done," they reiterated, "before daylight."

The Sister Superior was the mainspring of the hospital. She really was a wonderful person, small and insignificant to look at, except for her eyes, which looked you through and through and weighed you in the balance; absolutely true and straight, with a heart of gold, and the very calmest person in all the world. I remember her, late one evening, when everybody was rather agitated at a message which had come to say that 400 patients were on their way to the hospital, and room could only be made for 200 at the most. "Never mind," she said, not in the least perturbed, "they must be made as comfortable as possible on stretchers for the night, and to-morrow we must get some of the others moved away." And the Sisters took their cue from her, and those 400 patients were all taken in and looked after with less fuss than the arrival of forty unexpected patients in most hospitals.

All night long that procession of shattered men brought in on stretchers never ceased. The kitchen Sister stayed up all night so that each man should have some hot soup on arrival, and all the other Sisters were at their posts. Each man was undressed on the stretcher (often so badly wounded that all his clothing had to be cut off him) and hastily examined by the doctor. He was then dressed in a clean cotton shirt and trousers and lifted into bed, either to enjoy a bowl of hot soup, or, if the case was urgent, to be taken off in his turn to the operating-room. And though she was no longer young and not at all strong, there was dear Sister Superior herself all night, taking round the big bowls of soup or sitting beside the dying patients to cheer and comfort their last hours. How the men loved her.

It was she who gave the whole tone to the hospital—there the patients and their welfare were the first consideration and nothing else mattered in comparison. The hospital was not "smart" or "up to date," the wards were not even tidy, the staff was inadequate, overworked, and villainously housed, the resources very scanty, but for sheer selflessness and utter devotion to their work the staff of that hospital from top to bottom could not have been surpassed. I never heard a grumble or a complaint all the time I was there either from a doctor, a Sister, or an orderly, and I never saw in this hospital a dressing slurred over, omitted, or done without the usual precautions however tired or overworked everybody might be.

Of course the art of nursing as practised in England does not exist in Russia—even the trained Sisters do things every hour that would horrify us in England. One example of this is their custom of giving strong narcotic or stimulating drugs indiscriminately, such as morphine, codeine, camphor, or ether without doctors' orders. When untrained Sisters and inexperienced dressers do this (which constantly happens) the results are sometimes very deplorable. I have myself seen a dresser give a strong hypodermic stimulant to a man with a very serious hæmorrhage. The bleeding vessel was deep down and very difficult to find, and the hæmorrhage became so severe after the stimulant that for a long time his life was despaired of from extreme exhaustion due to loss of blood. I have also heard a Sister with no training except the two months' war course say she had given a certain man ten injections of camphor within an hour because he was so collapsed, but she had not seen fit to tell the doctor she had done this, nor had she let him know his patient was so much worse until he was at the point of death. Neither of these particular incidents could have happened in the Red Cross hospital at Warsaw as the Sisters there were properly trained; but even there they gave drugs at their own sweet will without consulting anyone—particularly in the night.

We were so busy at the hospital that we did not see much of Warsaw. To the casual observer it looks a busy, modern, rather gay capital, but almost every inch of the city is interesting historically, and nearly all the pages of that history are red with blood. War, revolutions, and riots seem to have been almost its normal condition, and the great broad Vistula that flows sluggishly through it has been many a time before stained crimson with the blood of its citizens. But this time the war is being fought under different conditions. Russians and Poles are for the first time working together with a common aim in view. If the only outcome of this war was the better mutual understanding of these two great nations, it would not have been fought entirely in vain.

When we first arrived the Russians had beaten the Germans back to the frontier, and every one was elated with the great victory. Now at the end of October things did not look quite so happy. The people who knew looked anxious and harassed. The newspapers, as usual, told nothing at all, but the news which always filters in somehow from mouth to mouth was not good. Terrific fighting was going on outside Lodz, it was said, and enormous German reinforcements were being poured in. Warsaw was full to overflowing with troops going through to reinforce on the Russian side. A splendid set of men they looked, sturdy, broad-chested, and hardy—not in the least smart, but practical and efficient in their warm brown overcoats and big top boots.

There are two things one notices at once about the Russian soldier. One is his absolute disregard of appearances. If he is cold he will tie a red comforter round his head without minding in the least whether he is in the most fashionable street in Warsaw or in camp at the front. The other noticeable characteristic is the friendly terms he is on with his officers. The Prussian soldiers rarely seem to like their officers, and it is not to be wondered at, as they treat their men in a very harsh, overbearing way. On duty the Russian discipline is strict, but off duty an officer may be heard addressing one of his men as "little pigeon" or "comrade" and other terms of endearment, and the soldier, on the other hand, will call his officer "little father" or "little brother." I remember one most touching scene when a soldier servant accompanied his wounded officer to hospital. The officer was quite a young, delicate-looking boy, who had been shot through the chest. His servant was a huge, rough Cossack, who would hardly let any of us touch his master if he could help it, and stayed by his bed night and day till the end, when, his great frame heaving with sobs and tears streaming down the seamed and rugged face, he threw himself over the officer's body and implored God to let him die too.

The hospital began to grow empty and the work slackened down, as every possible patient was sent away to Moscow or Petrograd to make room for the rush of wounded that must be coming from the Lodz direction. But no patients arrived, and we heard that the railway communications had been cut. But this proved to be untrue.

One Sunday afternoon Sister G. and I, being free, betook ourselves to tea at the Hotel d'Europe—that well-named hostelry which has probably seen more history made from its windows than any other hotel in Europe. We favoured it always on Sunday when we could, for not only was a particularly nice tea to be had, but one could also read there a not too old French newspaper. I think just at first we felt almost as cut off from news of what was happening on the English side as we did in Belgium. No English or French papers could be bought and the Polish and Russian papers were as sealed books to us, and when I did succeed in getting some long-suffering person to translate them to me, the news was naturally chiefly of the doings of the Russian side. Later on I had English papers sent out to me which kept me in touch with the western front, and also by that time, too, I could make out the substance of the Russian papers; but just at first it was very trying not to know what was going on. We had had tea and had read of an Anglo-French success near Ypres and returned rested and cheered to the hospital to find Sister Superior asking for us. She had had a message from the Red Cross Office that we were to go to Lodz next day, and were to go at once to the Hotel Bristol to meet Prince V., who would give us full particulars.

We went off at once to the Bristol and saw Prince V., but did not get any particulars—that was not the Prince's way. He was sitting reading in the lounge when we arrived, a very tall, lean, handsome man with kind brown eyes and a nose hooked like an eagle's. He greeted us very kindly and said he would take us to Lodz next day in one of the Red Cross automobiles, and that we must be ready at 10 A. M. I think we earned his everlasting gratitude by asking no questions as to where and how we were going to work, but simply said we would be ready at that time and returned to hospital to pack, fully realizing what lucky people we were to be going right into the thick of things, and only hoping that we should rise to the occasion and do the utmost that was expected of us.

We were now officially transferred from the hospital to the Flying Column, of which Prince V. was the head. A flying column works directly under the head of the Red Cross, and is supposed to go anywhere and do anything at any hour of the day or night. Our Column consisted of five automobiles that conveyed us and all our equipment to the place where we were to work, and then were engaged in fetching in wounded, and taking them on to the field hospital or ambulance train. The staff consisted of Prince and Princess V., we two English Sisters, with generally, but not always, some Russian ones in addition, an English surgeon, Colonel S., some Russian dressers and students, and some sanitars, or orderlies. The luggage was a dreadful problem, and the Prince always groaned at the amount we would take with us, but we could not reduce it, as we had to carry big cases of cotton-wool, bandages and dressings, anæsthetics, field sterilizer, operating-theatre equipment, and a certain amount of stores—such as soap, candles, benzine and tinned food—as the column would have been quite useless if it had not been to a large extent self-supporting. Our Column was attached to the Second Army, which operated on the eastern front of Warsaw. The Russian front changes so much more rapidly than the Anglo-French front, where progress is reckoned in metres, that these mobile columns are a great feature of ambulance work here. Our front changed many miles in a week sometimes, so that units that can move anywhere at an hour's notice are very useful. The big base hospitals cannot quite fulfil the same need on such a rapidly changing front.

EXCERPTS OF CHAPTERS FROM
Field Hospital and Flying Column, 1915

Printed in Great Britain
by Amazon